THE 20-MINUTE
NETWORKING MEETING

Veterans Edition

The 20-Minute Networking Meeting - Veterans Edition

SILVER: Foreword INDIES Book of the Year - Career
FINALIST: National Indies Excellence Awards - Career
FINALIST: International Book Awards - Career

ALSO FROM CAREER INNOVATIONS PRESS

The 20-Minute Networking Meeting - Executive Edition

The 20-Minute Networking Meeting - Graduate Edition
WINNER: USA Best Book Award - College Guides Category

and

The 20-Minute Networking Meeting - Professional Edition
WINNER: International Book Awards - Business - Career
WINNER: National Indie Excellence Award - Career
SILVER: Axiom Business Book Award - Career
FINALIST: USA Best Book Award - Career
FINALIST: Foreword INDIES Book of the Year - Career

The
20-Minute
Networking
Meeting

VETERANS EDITION

Learn to Network. Get a Job.

NATHAN A. PEREZ
and MARCIA BALLINGER, PhD

CAREER INNOVATIONS PRESS

Volume book orders are available at a discount.
Contact Career Innovations Press for more information.
www.20mnm.com

Published 2019 by Career Innovations Press.
Cover design by Linda Koutsky
Interior design by Linda Koutsky

ISBN-978-0-9859106-9-3

Marcia would like to dedicate this book to:
her husband, Brad and her daughter, Analisa.

* * *

Nathan would like to dedicate this book to his father
Severo S Perez, Navy (Ret); Peter S Duran, Navy; Santiago S Perez, Marines; Arturo S Perez, Army; José A Perez, Air Force; Christopher D Perez, Army; Rudy R Perez, Marines; Alberto Alvarez, Air Force; Archie T Spillman, Air Force; Eldon R Spillman, Navy

Francisco R Trujillo, Army, POW - WWII, Germany; José R Trujillo, Army; Manuel R Trujillo, Navy; Mathias R Garcia, Army; Mike R Trujillo, Army; Ramon R Trujillo, Army; Raymond A Trujillo, Army; Joseph D Moralez, Navy
Robert R Woods, Marines; James E Gregg, Air Force; Frank X Garcia, Marines; Brendan Cain, Air Force

Contents

Acknowledgments

The 20-Minute Networking Meeting is rooted in two core values: Collaboration and Community. We believe that a successful organization (and a successful individual!) needs to care about a wide variety of constituencies and stakeholders and to treat each other with concern and respect.

One way that Collaboration and Community come into play is in the networking we, as recruitment professionals, do with people in job transition. Even when we are not working on a related search, we seek to assist each person who contacts us by sharing information with them, offering helpful suggestions, or perhaps, giving a word of encouragement.

Of course, a book like this that stresses the importance of relationships couldn't be possible without the help, insight, and contributions of others. We would like to acknowledge the wisdom and generosity of a few friends and colleagues from the veteran and non-veteran communities.

In particular, Nathan would like to recognize U.S. Army veteran, Alan Hill. Alan was instrumental to the introductions of people and resources that give this book its veteran perspective. Many other veterans and business professionals provided their own job-search perspectives on *what it is like out there* and took the time to meet and share their experiences with us as well. Thank you to Eric Ahlness; Paul Anderson; Kurtis Anderson; Erika Cashin; Tom Colosimo; Bob Dixon; Delilah Duran; Annette Euresti; Robert Frias; Elizabeth Garcia; Curt Gilbert; Beth Glassman; Pam Golos; Sam Graber; Les Hoffman; Sheila Jessen; Stephen Kolcinski; Mark Lindquist; Adam Naryka; Mike Orren; Chris Passaro; Stuart Perelmuter; Jessica A. Perez; Margie Trujillo Rocha; Russell Schmidt; Gustavo Strasser; Santiago Strasser; Lisa Troen; Julie Wells; Adam Widder; Aaron Zaslofsky; and Linda Koutsky for her beautiful book design.

PART I

Introduction

(Or: Read Me So The Book Makes Sense)

Welcome to *The 20-Minute Networking Meeting!* The information contained in this book *will* revolutionize the way you think about networking, whether you're looking for post-service employment, or are proactively managing your civilian career. Meeting with jobseekers every day, we've observed what works in networking—from the hiring side of the desk. Consequently, we've also observed what does not work, and sadly, the vast majority of networking meetings are near-complete failures. *The 20-Minute Networking Meeting - Veterans Edition* is meant to remedy that, and to help you develop a civilian-ready skill set that is arguably the most important in business: networking.

The 20-Minute Networking Meeting deconstructs this networking process to show what job-search networking looks like from your *contacts'* perspectives. Following its lessons and advice, you will learn to conduct meetings that those contacts find valuable, engaging, and impressive—all inside twenty minutes. Written by two career professionals with a combined networking experience of over 50 years, the material in this book is designed with *you*, a veteran, in mind. *Everything* in it is relevant to your situation as a job-seeker—even if your networking skills or professional experience is limited.

The *Veterans Edition* includes the stories and perspectives of fellow veterans, career experts, hiring professionals, and business executives from across a broad set of industries. The inclusion of such diverse professional experiences are meant to not only give you insight into what to expect during *your* networking journeys, but with multiple professional perspectives, teach you how to prepare for it *now*.

So don't skip ahead. Having a full understanding of the *20MNM* model is imperative to your job-seeking success. Mastering it will affect far more than just getting your first or next job after serving. It will impact the rest of your career.

Let's get on with it.

A Couple of
Networking Stories...

Penny & Mitchell

Penny looked at her calendar. It was going to be a busy day of meetings. Her first, she noted, was a networking meeting with Mitchell Lennox at her sister's request. He was a Navy veteran. Penny didn't know as much about veterans as Cheryl, but they had family members who had been in the military. Neighbors, too. Of course she would help.

Though CTE had no available jobs for Mitchell at moment, this was just a networking meeting. Besides, she knew that she could connect him with other people, both in and out of the company, even though her job had nothing to do with recruitment. Her network of professionals had already led to employment for almost a dozen veterans to date, and she was confident they could help Mitchell, too.

On the hour, Penny grabbed a notebook and left for the lobby to find Mitchell. As she walked by her boss's office, he called out. There was a group conference call in one hour, he announced. About the sales group.

"Alright," she replied.

She walked away with a quicker pace. Sales was her group. That meant she had to be there. He didn't gather people at the last moment for nothing, so something was up.

She was hurrying now. The call was not expected, and she wondered how she needed to prepare. She would need time. She would need to get Mitchell's meeting started immediately.

"Mitchell? Nice to meet you!" she said, holding out her hand as she crossed the lobby. He smiled down at her warmly and shook it.

"Nice to meet you too, ma'am. You can call me Mitch," he said, quickly grabbing his things to follow her out of the lobby.

Penny led him down a hallway and began their discussion to get ahead of time.

"Did you find the building okay? Parking alright?"

"Yes, ma'am. Easy to find. Parking was fine, thank you."

Polite. Formal. Friendly, too, but didn't look at her.

Penny chose the closest conference room. Sensing her urgency, Mitchell pulled a resume from his folder as she closed the door.

"How has the job search been?" she asked, taking it from him and seating herself. Penny scanned the resume, then glanced up at the clock. They were past ten minutes already. Get going, she told herself.

"Pretty rough, to be honest, ma'am," Mitchell replied with a chuckle. "Doesn't seem like there's a lot for vets, and getting calls on what's leftover is pretty infrequent. I don't even really hear back about applications or emails I send. So," he smiled again. "Not great."

His candor caught Penny off guard. She knew a lot of veterans felt this way, but she was never sure how to talk about it. She knew it was an issue on both sides of the hiring desk, and she heard about it all the time, even outside of her company. But she didn't know what to do about that, either. Except what she was doing now—meeting with him, with the intention to help.

She scanned his resume again. A lot of terminology. She wished she was better at reading services acronyms. Her HR work was in benefits and compensation, and interpreting resumes, much less military resumes, was not part of her job, and certainly not a strength.

Not a problem, though, she thought. He could probably do that for her.

"How about just tell me about what you do, or what your biggest experiences are?" Penny suggested.

Mitchell sat back.

"Oh," he said. He was caught off guard this time. But he recovered and smiled confidently. "Well, anything cyber," he said. "I like it a lot, and I'm really good at it. Especially cyber security." He gestured at his resume. "I can answer any question that you have."

That *was* the question I had, Penny thought, smiling back.

She wished Mitchell would give her more detail or explanation; incomplete answers weren't going to get them anywhere.

Penny grimaced. This is where she got bogged down in networking meetings. Interviewing was something recruiters and hiring managers did, not her, but she didn't know a better way to get information than her own question-asking.

But then it hit her—why am *I* asking questions in the first place? Wasn't it Mitch who was seeking information? Wasn't this his meeting?

She was getting frustrated. Another glance at the clock. Go!

"Here's the thing, Mitch—" she said. "I know nothing about cyber security. *But,* if you can tell me what you're especially good at, or what kind of work you're seeking, maybe I can think of where to send you or where to look."

Mitch tensed, but maintained his confident smile.

"Really, I'm good at *all* of it, ma'am," he said assuringly. "I can do nearly any kind of computer work you have here or anywhere. And I'm not picky, I just want a job."

Penny pushed back in her seat. This was a non-starter. "*I just want a job,*" was not what employers were looking to hear, and his non-specifics was giving her nowhere to go with their discussion. How was she going to help him?

But it was obvious that Mitch didn't know this. He just wasn't aware of it yet.

This concerned her. Though this was not his fault, Mitchell's approach would greatly impact his meetings, including any people she might introduce him to. That could be a problem. Was this why he was having trouble in his job search?

Penny decided that maybe she shouldn't be asking Mitchell questions to begin with.

"How about I answer anything *you* want to know instead?" she laughed. "Maybe if I do that, you'll get more from our time together."

But his reaction confirmed that he wasn't expecting to ask questions at all that day. "Right," he said, shifting in his chair.

It made her wonder: had he not thought to ask questions during *any* of his meetings?

"Well, could you tell me more about what you guys do here at CTE?" he asked.

Penny stared at him in surprise. Did he not *already* know? Had he not looked at the website?

"No, ma'am, I didn't," he chuckled. "Just so busy meeting people these last few weeks. I kinda figured you were the best person to tell me since we were gonna meet anyway." He gave that confident, friendly smile again.

There was a knock on the door and it swung open. Her co-worker, wearing a regretful expression on her face whispered

"Sorry! We're doing it now, Penny, they're moving the call to now…" and closed the door again.

Penny turned back to Mitch. It all happened very fast, but she could see that Mitch already understood that their meeting was at an end. His expression fell.

"Sorry, Mitch," Penny said. "This was unexpected for me as well."

He began to speak quickly. "Do you know of any jobs here?" he asked. It was the longest he held eye contact with her. She felt terrible for having to say no.

"I'm not sure yet what you're looking for," Penny said. "And unfortunately there's nothing here right now anyway."

"How about any other companies?" he asked. "I mean, since you work in HR, maybe you hear of things?"

She shook her head. Knowing such things wasn't part of her day-to-day job, either. Had he looked at her LinkedIn profile or company bio, he would have known all this before the meeting.

There was an awkward silence, but this time she didn't know how to fill it. I know a handful of other people he might contact, she thought. But he doesn't seem prepared enough to meet them. And she wasn't sure she wanted to endorse him at this time anyway; he didn't seem able to express his professional experience to non-veterans like her yet, and that would be important for her network of people—they would likely get confused, too. Still, she wanted to help somehow, some way.

"Well, maybe we can at least stay in touch," Penny proposed, standing up. "If something comes up, I'd be happy to reach out."

He stood up with her. His expression reflected disappointment. Mitchell clearly understood that this meeting hadn't turned out the way either of them had intended. But in a final show of professionalism, he held out his hand.

"Thank you, ma'am, for your time," he said, as she shook it.

"And yes, please do keep me in mind."

Mitchell grabbed his things, and Penny walked him to the reception area. On the way out, she glanced once more at the clock. Almost twenty-five minutes with Mitchell Lennox, and while they had discussed a few things, they'd accomplished nothing.

Now let's take a look at a networking meeting that went a little differently.

Jake & Maggie

Jake dropped into his chair and pulled up his calendar. With the end of tax season coming, he was finally seeing the light at the end of the tunnel. At the same time, it was getting busier than ever as the April 15 deadline approached. On his to-do list today: pluck out more of his clients' W2s from an eight-inch stack of mail and return at least a dozen calls before five. Then there was email. And daily review meetings to prep for.

His phone rang. Jake leaned back and picked up the handset.

"Good morning, this is Jake," he answered far more relaxed than he felt.

"Jake, it's Maggie. I'm at the Starbucks down the street and thought I'd bring you a coffee for our nine o'clock meeting."

Jake sat up and studied the calendar again. Maggie? Her name was there, but her face was missing from his mind. Had he made this appointment?

"Jake, did I lose you?"

"A latte would be fantastic; thank you for offering," he responded, still in a relaxed tone. If she was polite enough to offer, he would be polite enough to accept. But he gritted his teeth. How had this happened? How had he scheduled something in the busiest time of year?

"Latte it is," Maggie said. "See you in a few minutes."

Ten minutes later, Jake showed her into his office, closing the door behind them. Her name was ringing a bell now, but he was still wracking his brain to place her face. He felt terrible that he would have to admit this. Worse, he didn't know if he could commit to an hour for an unplanned meeting.

"Thank you again for taking the time to meet, Jake," Maggie said as she placed her coffee on the table. "I know this is your busy season, so I won't keep you long."

Jake also set down his coffee, and sat across from her with a tense smile.

"Just a reminder as to our connection," Maggie continued, settling herself in. "Marion Ambrose, who sends her greetings, suggested I reach out to you. It was a few weeks ago. She warned that you were about to hit tax season, but insisted that we might be able to help each other network. So, thank you, again, for your time."

Marion! thought Jake, letting out a subtle sigh of relief. It finally came back to him. Marion was an old college friend who was in the ROTC at the time; some kind of reserve officer program. She mentioned Maggie at a gathering months ago. Maggie was about to leave the service and was looking for a job in finance or accounting. He knew he wouldn't have scheduled Maggie if it wasn't important, but now that he realized it was a networking meeting, he wished he would have waited till after the 15th. He could hear emails rolling in behind him even as they sat there, and his phone had silently buzzed twice.

"But even though we're networking," Maggie went on as though reading his mind, "I'll only take twenty minutes of your time."

Twenty minutes. He'd heard that before. She had good intentions, he was sure, but what she meant was an hour, and he didn't have that. He glanced at the clock again. Their meeting had to start now.

"Here is my situation," Maggie said, one step ahead. She opened her folder. "I'm a few months out of the service, and making a transition into the civilian workforce. However, I'm not asking for a job. I'm doing research on possible career directions."

Eli, Jake's assistant, poked his nose in the door.

"Jake, a reminder about these forms," he said, putting a stack on Jake's desk. "They have to be signed and overnighted by 10 A.M."

Eli left, and Jake stared at the documents. Mail pick up was an hour and blocks away. If this meeting with Maggie was like any other, he wouldn't get them out on time.

"No problem with time, Jake," Maggie said, reading his thoughts again. "I promised—only twenty minutes."

She jumped right back in.

"I met Marion through her daughter, who is my best friend. Audra and I went to high school together. After graduation, Audra left to earn her bachelor's in finance while I joined the Army. We stayed in touch, and I learned a lot about her civilian job search along the way. If you didn't know, Audra got multiple job offers even before graduating. She said it had everything to do with her relationship-building, and the information she gathered from other people along the way. So networking was clearly the way to go, which is how I got here."

Maggie's demeanor was steady. She didn't come off as negative or apologetic, or even very nervous. Jake admired her attitude. Job search was not easy. He knew by experience. And having met with many veterans over the years, he knew that job search could be even more challenging for those right out of active duty or with little professional experience. But Maggie seemed comfortable despite these circumstances.

"In the Army," she continued. "I was a Financial Management Technician. As you probably know, the military uses titles that can sound pretty different than non-military titles, but my job was more or less in receivables. I received, reviewed, and processed checks for payment; received and reviewed third-party contracts; and invoiced, and maintained disbursing files for all the above. And while I think I'd like to find a role doing similar work, I'd like to focus my questions on your perceptions of other possible career paths."

Jake hesitated. Career direction. He wasn't sure he was the right person to give answers on that. Especially for military veterans. Their backgrounds were so different than more traditional ones, or so it seemed.

But again, Maggie seemed to read his thoughts.

"I've been asking several people these same questions. Different perspectives on the same thing are important, and I would really value your insights."

He glanced at the clock again. He was sure this is where things would get out of hand. A "question or two" usually turned into a scattered conversation with no direction. But he gave her the benefit of the doubt. She seemed to have a handle on what she wanted out of the meeting.

"Sure, go for it," Jake said.

Maggie asked Jake about growth areas that he was seeing with his clients. Were things changing? Was that influencing the financial industry on a broader basis? Did he foresee anything that would make the accounting world different?

If this is what Maggie really wanted to know, the past several weeks had given Jake plenty to talk about in terms of industry trends. He shared high points over the next ten minutes. As he did, Maggie busily scribbled notes in her notebook, asking clarifying questions along the way. Jake grinned pleasantly in spite of being stressed about time. She was taking him seriously, and had obviously done research about subjects that he could talk about. It made their meeting more conversational, and he felt like he was able to actually help her out as a result.

Once he finished his final thought, Maggie tapped her pen on her notebook.

"I think you've answered my other questions," she smiled. "Thank you! Can you think of someone else I could ask these same kinds of questions as part of my research?"

He'd been asked this before. Usually it was uncomfortable giving out names, but Maggie had her act together. She clearly knew what she was seeking, did her research, managed their time, and showed gratitude for being there. He understood now why Marion had insisted she reach out, and he didn't hesitate to give her a name.

"Thaddeus Bryant," he said. Thad would appreciate Maggie's sharp and together approach. He was a good referral for her, too. "Thad has worked in finance for years, and knows everyone in financial circles in the city. In fact, he helped me out. Go ahead and use my name. He's an old friend and long-term client. Also, he's a veteran. I think he can give you some solid advice about how to use your military finance skills in the business world. He's done it for years."

Maggie wrote down the information and smiled. What a bonus. Someone in business with a service background—and knew the civilian ropes!

She closed her folder and put away her pen.

"Thank you so much, Jake. That's all I have. As I said, I want to be respectful of your schedule. But one last question: How can

I be helpful to you?"

Jake leaned back. What jobseeker asks a question like this?

" . . . uh, I can't think of anything at the moment, if I'm honest . . ."

"No problem! Reading your LinkedIn profile, I saw that you consult entrepreneurs on financial matters. One of my mentors is another veteran, and is a partner with an organization called Vetrepreneur. They coach and advise potential veteran entrepreneurs. If you are interested, I would be happy to introduce you if you think that would be beneficial. I know they could use a speaker and a resource for all things financial."

Jake found himself smiling again. He had read about that organization and all the good things they were doing. It would be a great relationship, if not client, to have.

"That would be wonderful, thank you, Maggie."

She smiled and stood up, extending her hand. He shook it.

"Thank you again, Jake," she said. "It was a pleasure to meet you."

He walked her to the door. A quick glance at the clock showed that he still had forty minutes to sign and mail out his docs. She had actually stuck to twenty minutes.

"I'll be sure to tell Marion hello for you once I let her know we had a chance to meet," Maggie said. "Have a great rest of the week!"

"You too, Maggie. And thank you again for the coffee!"

This Book Is for *You*

You could probably relate to some part of the previous two stories. As you saw, some networking meetings go a little more smoothly (not to mention more effectively) than others. But it's not just chance or luck that determines whether a networking meeting goes well. It's skill—skill that can be learned and perfected with process and practice. This book will break down the successful networking meeting into its essential parts and give you the tools needed to make your own powerful meetings. Before that though, here is bit of necessary background on why the *The 20-Minute Networking Meeting* model was built.

Both authors of this book are retained executive search firm professionals. Executive search firms are hired by other companies to find new executive leaders for their organizations. As recruiting professionals, we're something like hiring managers for the *company*, at the executive level.

Because of the nature of the industry, recruiters, along with company hiring managers, are contacted literally every day to network as part of someone's job search. It's a sensible step in any jobseeker's strategy, but we have come to dread this oft-repeated request, regardless of how much we appreciate meeting these bright individuals.

"Hello. This is Susan SuperExec. I was referred to you because I'm looking for a new job. I'm networking, and I want to meet with you."

Why dread these meetings when these talented professionals are our bread and butter? Because the meetings are almost always ineffective. In fact, some are *so* ineffective that it would have been better if the jobseeker had not called at all. And other meetings, while adequate enough, simply miss their full potential. And these are *executives* we're talking about—people who hold meetings as part of their daily business lives.

Over time, it became apparent what was consistently going wrong in such important meetings. It also became apparent what was going right. What was ultimately observed was that the very foundation of the networking meeting was being overlooked entirely. Potentially terrific networking meetings were suffering fatal blows. Those meetings were not well planned, well run, or even meaningful. They *certainly* didn't have mutuality or gratitude.

After sharing these notes with hiring and recruitment peers—people who are also frequently asked to network—they overwhelmingly agreed that most networking meetings are entirely too long, problematic, and ineffective. Thus, *The 20-Minute Networking Meeting* editions of books.

The 20-Minute Networking Meeting - Veterans Edition is written from a hiring and recruiting perspective, and will tell you what works for the people you are contacting and hoping to impress on the civilian side of things. Step-by-step, we will analyze the structure of successful networking meetings and show you how you can put the *20MNM* model to work for yourself.

Now let's take a look at why networking is so crucial for a job-search.

Why Networking Is So Important

(Or: Hey, Friend, Your Job Market Is Hiding from You)

If you did not already know, in spite of the huge number of online tools for civilian jobseekers, most roles are *not* filled by online resume services or community job boards.

So where does one find those jobs? In the *invisible* job market, of course!

Whether you've heard of it or not, that's what it's called, and yes, it does exist. The invisible (or hidden) job market consists of job openings that are not advertised or publicly posted. These positions are filled by (or sometimes created for) candidates who come to an employer's attention through employee recommendations (like friends who already have jobs); referrals from trusted associates (friends; family; professional contacts), recruiters, or direct contact with the candidates who may be interviewing for these jobs (such as you).

And where would this invisible job market *be*?

You're standing in it. It's all around you, all the time. It's there when you pick up your phone and when you send an email. In fact, it's literally the *rumor* of job opportunities that you've heard about, well before seeing them posted somewhere. And get this— it's estimated that a whopping 70-80% of *all* jobs are obtained through people you know!

So how does one *become* part of the invisible job market, you ask?

Occasionally through recruiters or hiring managers like us. And the Invisible Dimension portal. That one's hard to find, though, so networking is your better bet.

Networking, you say with a grimace. ***Does it really come down to networking?***

Yes, it does. But the good news is that it's easier than you think. Networking, to the casual practitioner, is all about *who* you know, rather than *what* you know. While there's truth to that, it doesn't tell the whole story. The reality is if you haven't developed networking skills, then who you know simply won't matter. In fact, undeveloped networking skills will be the leading cause of closed doors and unanswered calls. *Build* this networking skill and you'll gain additional skills, valuable contacts and information that will take you anywhere you want to go. That's not conjecture. That's tried and true by some of the most admired leaders in business. And it will be the same for you.

◇◇

TIP
The longer you maintain a healthy network,
the more powerful it becomes each passing day. Take
advantage of it *now* and empower your future.

◇◇

What It is, What It Does, and Why It Works

While this book's information is applicable to all kinds of networking, we're going to focus on the topic as it relates to jobseekers. The next statement sums up the importance of establishing a vibrant network:

No one is going to hire you if no one knows you exist. Right? Right.

But your chances increase tenfold if you've at least been *introduced* to a hiring authority by a friend, family member, neighbor or service peer(s) (shipmate; airman; buddy; team; staff or other service colleagues)—or perhaps even by someone you've just *met*. Agreed?

If you know one person, and that person knows another, then you have a valid and working (however small) network. Imagine if your network included *dozens* of people. Or hundreds. (Entirely possible, as you'll read later.) With a network this large, you could certainly achieve your goals. You would surely find out about the invisible job market. And there's no doubt you'd find out who's hiring.

But let's take a closer look at how that works.

Loosely defined, networking is the practice of meeting with other people with a specific purpose in mind. In your case, that purpose would be to obtain information that leads to your first or next job after serving. Simple as that.

I've mentioned that this practice is imperative to job search in the civilian workforce. Whether you are someone returning to the workforce after a long period of time due to the armed services, or even personal reasons, networking becomes that much *more* important to you.

Which returns us to basics, and the reason why: people want to know who you are if they are going to offer you time and information. *Personally*. It involves basic trust. No amount of social networking or LinkedIn connections will ever replace *personal* relationship building. Nor is there any cover letter or well-crafted resume that's going to get the job (hunt) done better or faster. And while there are job boards, advertisements, online applications, mailed inquiries, and other such virtual job-search methods, will such opportunities be in your field of experience, or things you'd even be interested in?

Odds are slim.

But for the sake of argument, let's say you *do* find something online. Can you imagine the hundreds of other applicants you'd be competing with just to be *looked* at? It suddenly makes the idea of finding a magic portal more appealing, doesn't it?

Which takes us back to networking, the next best thing.

I mentioned earlier that 70% of all jobs are awarded only in the hidden job market. If you aspire to be a business leader, that figure jumps to 80% because there are even less company leadership roles available. So, if 70-80% of jobs are obtained through networking (which is the same as saying are *not posted!*), doesn't it make sense to spend the same amount of your time focused on face-to-face activities?

Resumes and application submissions often end up in a review pile, if not a recycle pile, and that does no good.

So what must be done? You must get on your feet. You must network.

When it comes to hiring, all resumes must be sifted and studied. There are piles, there are those who sift through piles, and there are the weeks, and sometimes months it can take to do so. It is typically a slow process, and—truth be told—even the hiring and recruitment side want it to go faster. This is why face-to-face meetings are simply the fastest way to cut ahead of the competition. Even for those looking to *recruit or hire!* Efficient, to the point, with contact. *Networking*.

In general, such a respectful, brief approach to meetings is appreciated by nearly *every* professional, as time limitation is often what determines most people's scheduling.

Try not to take this for granted. And try to remember that time management in the business world does not behave like or work with military precision. There is an ebb and flow in daily business that cannot be controlled by people, and therefore makes time management a constant challenge for everyone, all the time. It's for this reason that people appreciate what we're talking about here—a structured meeting process. Especially networking meetings. Maintaining and leveraging situational awareness when it comes to the above, will go a very long way in your job search. It will certainly make you visible in the invisible job market.

Here's some more good news: you already have a functioning network! Remember, every person you know is in it. And every person you meet expands it. *Everyone*. Being a veteran, veteran career groups can grow your networking circle even faster. And with so many who came before you, you have an almost endless resource of civilian-experienced veterans that can be found in all industries, professions, and corners of the country. All you have to do is get out there, look, and reach out!

But *wait, wait,* you say. If 70-80% of my search work should be face-to-face meetings, what about the other 20-30% of my time?

Glad you asked. Online postings are a great place to "see what's out there," but still a second choice to in-person networking. If you *must* use the web, use your 20-30% time searching those online postings. A better idea, however, would be to use that time to correspond via email and follow up with brief thank-yous for those completed face-to-face meetings.

POTENTIAL NETWORKING CONTACTS:

- Your transition office
- Service peers and colleagues (shipmate; wingman; buddy; team; squad; staff)
- Fellow veterans - any branch (and age)
- Former co-workers, peers, and staff from previous employers
- Professionals, veterans, or others you've met at trade associations, conferences, or training programs
- Professional trade groups
- Friends, neighbors, and members of your faith community
- Fellow alumni from the high school, college(s) or trade school(s) you attended
- Fraternities and Sororities
- Vendors, suppliers, and clients you've worked with
- Consultants you've worked with
- Career guidance counselors from your current/former college or university (Note: Often there are *alumni* services, too, so you don't need to be a current student to take advantage of the help!)
- Fellow members of academic, civic and athletic clubs (Former athlete? Teammates and coaches are a great place to start!)
- Professional service providers, such as your financial planner; attorney; and tax preparer
- Chambers of Commerce
- State; County; or City Workforce employment centers (which oftentimes have special veteran services)

IMPORTANT NOTE:

The boxed examples are only meant to be a "jump start" in building your contact base. There is no limit to how wide your network can grow. You'll keep adding new names to your network as you meet new people.

Also, don't forget that there are many networking groups designed specifically for your background and profession. Take a moment to find such groups through LinkedIn or even your alma mater's Career Services or Alumni Relations office or website. Barring those options, and as mentioned above, many city and/or counties maintain Workforce Centers. They are designed to help jobseekers find employment for themselves. Just hop on the web for a look!

How Networking (*Really*) Works

As mentioned a few times already, most jobs are filled by contacts that come from personal relationships. This isn't necessarily the same as saying friendships or long term acquaintances. It's just people that we have met or know to some degree. And whether intentional or not, it's the common approach in business. For instance, a strong recommendation from a trusted source (i.e. friend; family member; former co-worker, or in your case, service peer/colleague) could be all that's needed for you to get an interview with a hiring manager. Decision-makers look to *their* networks for valued suggestions and referrals, too. And as there's no way someone can *know* a candidate by reading a piece of paper outlining a work history (resume), their contacts' trusted word is paramount. For example, when the search for an employee starts, the first question a hiring decision-maker usually asks is:

"Hey—who do you know that can do this job?"

The answer, more often than not, is:

"Let me think about whom I know."

And *justlikethat*, the networking has begun. Don't you want to be the person who comes to mind right away?

Here's a scenario. Let's presume there are two potential candidates with similar service backgrounds. We'll call them Passive

Candidate and Active Candidate. Both were in the Army, both have related technological experience, both are getting into the same profession, and both are networking for similar jobs in the same city. Essentially, they're in the exact same circumstances, with the exact same qualifications.

Passive Candidate has been slow to start the networking process, focusing instead on combing the Internet and studying online postings and want ads. It's what's there, and it's what he knows how to do. He's comfortable taking it easy, and using this methodology, sets up a few networking meetings.

Active Candidate has put her time toward active networking. By phoning some former unit buddies, sending out emails to contacts (civilian *and* veteran) at some companies and organizations, and scheduling lunches with several employed friends, Active Candidate succeeds in conducting twenty-five networking meetings. (Remember—*anyone* you know is in your network. And as everyone knows someone else, your contact base can easily add up to more than twenty-five people.)

Now Active Candidate and Passive Candidate are quickly on two different paths.

Just to make things interesting, though, let's say that Active Candidate didn't feel too hot about the result of some of her meetings. It hampers some of her efforts, and consequently her confidence. We'll come back to this again in a second.

Okay, to recap what we have so far: two people, similar background, same set of circumstances, two different approaches, and a number of networking meetings. Now let's develop the invisible job market to see how they do.

Switch to the perspective of the hiring manager who is looking to fill a new role. He has talked to those around him about the position—"Hey, who do you know that can do this job?"—and word has begun to spread through his trusted group (network) of peers, former colleagues, friends, and maybe even former unit buddies (whether around town or around the country). As it does, those people share this information with *their* network of peers, former colleagues, and friends, letting them know that a new job is up for grabs at ABC Company.

Voilà! Now you have a posting in the invisible job market.

With all the pieces on the table, it should be clear that Active Candidate has much more of an edge. But let's look more closely at how.

If *any* of those twenty-five people whom Active Candidate happened to meet with is in the extended network of the hiring manager, Active Candidate's going to hear word of the opportunity. Plain and simple. To be more specific, people talk, and people pass forward this kind of information. With each new person who learns of this new job, it can be surmised that the information will be disseminated to at least one, if not a few more people, until there is a widely cast net. Active Candidate is going to hear of the opportunity, *just by being in the network.*

By contrast, Passive Candidate likely doesn't even know the job *exists* yet. Why? Because it's not posted, and because it's less likely that Passive Candidate's smaller network overlaps with the hiring manager's extended network. (Yes, it's *possible*—just less likely.) So, without actively growing his network, Passive Candidate is going to miss an opportunity because he put more time into postings than people.

This should make it crystal clear how Active Candidate stands a pretty good chance of getting a face-to-face meeting with ABC Company. Agreed?

Now let's address Active Candidate's not-so-good meeting that we mentioned earlier, just so we can draw another networking point.

Let's say, for sake of our networking argument, that word

from the hiring manager has finally made its way through the grapevine to one of the people that Active Candidate met with. But for some reason that meeting didn't go well. Maybe it was bumpy, maybe someone was tired, or maybe the contact was somewhat reluctant to meet in the first place. (People have bad days.) Even if this were the case, Active Candidate has become an extension of the total network anyway. She immediately becomes the first qualified person to pop into her contact's head, bumpy meeting or not. That alone makes her *far* more likely to get the job than Passive Candidate, who is still at home basking in the glow of his computer screen. Wouldn't you say?

And *justlikethat*, Active Candidate has become visible in the invisible job market. Passive Candidate, on the other hand, simply wouldn't know better.

Becoming the Best
(Networker) You Can Be

Earlier, I stated that most of the networking meetings I participate in are ineffective. These are executives, mind you; people
who have had many years in the civilian workforce to master
them. The reason for the ineffectiveness is because many people in
job transition, executive or not, focus much of their attention on
LinkedIn profiles and resumes—how to write them; how to format them; which keywords to highlight; and how often to send or
share everything. By contrast, they don't think much about their
face-to-face meetings—the ONE thing that GETS jobs. And yet,
from a recruitment perspective, networking is where the major
problems are.

The fact is, you can tweak your resume from here to kingdom
come and it will not make much difference. After all, how perfectly written does a resume need to be before you get a call? How
many do you need to send out to get even one response? How
many LinkedIn connections must you have to get an
appointment?

But—what if you were to become an expert *networker*? Someone who is well informed and well regarded by a large group of

connections? (Like, for example, who you and your wingman, buddy, shipmate, team, squad, staff or other service colleagues are to each other.) Someone for whom each interaction is a job-seeking home run? Someone who has built a network that is actively engaged in helping YOU find your first or next great job? Now we're talking!

Here are the three things you want to get out of a networking meeting:

- Gather some new information
- Add new contacts to your list
- Gain an evangelist (Say what? Don't worry, I'll explain.)

Just what kind of new information are we talking about? A clearer understanding of what your job market is looking for and how you fit in that market, are a couple of examples.

For instance, how do your, MOCs/MOSs transfer to the corporate or civilian work world? Do your military communication skills translate to a specific human resources role? Emergency management systems? Advertising? Or maybe even all of the above? What about location? Can you find your kind of desired work someplace other than where you called home before serving? (Remember—opportunities abound, but might not be where you are or were.)

Get a handle on such information and you will quickly see how it not only impacts your job search, but your career choices, personal fulfillment, and quality of life.

That's nothing to sneeze at.

Before we take the jump, let's clear our networking path by debunking some networking myths.

Networking Myths

(Or: Never Ever Believe These Things)

Networking gets a pretty bad rap. This is often due to misperceptions and misunderstanding. Let's debunk some myths about networking and deconstruct some common mistakes. Here are some ways of thinking that you want to leave behind:

- I'm Just Wasting My Time
- Networking Is Just Schmoozing
- Networking Is Cheating
- No One Wants To Hear Me Talk About Myself
- No One Wants To Meet With A Veteran Or Inexperienced Worker
- The Longer The Meeting, The Better
- A Networking Meeting Is When I Give A Detailed Description Of My Background
- Off The Cuff Is Best; I'll Figure Out Each Meeting When I Get There
- People I Know Will Find Me A Job!

Now let's debunk them.

— MYTH —

"I'm Just Wasting My Time."

Pssst—remember the previous section? The part about how 70-80% of jobs are found through networking? Believe when I say that, from a hiring and recruiting perspective, it's no waste of time.

Meeting with people (both new and old contacts) is probably the most important thing you can do while looking for work. Your networking meetings could surely lead to job connections, but the networking meetings might lead to *other* opportunities that you hadn't yet thought about.

For instance, your meetings could get you caught up on happenings in your current or future industry—or maybe even introduce you to a new one. Or you might learn of *other* business opportunities such as contract or temporary work, or even *new professions* related to your background and experience that you never knew existed. That alone is a *life-changer!* And feedback? Absolutely. This in turn will sharpen your networking skill set, which in turn further improves your chances of obtaining your networking goals—including getting a job.

But these are just a *few* benefits of networking. So get rid of this mentality. Networking is never a waste of time.

— MYTH —

"Networking Is Just Schmoozing."

Mark this with a pen. Lots of people commit the sin of schmoozing. Shooting the breeze is enjoyable, but not if you're the person who has work piling up back at the office. Save the irrelevant chitchat. If you don't, you'll come across more as a social-minded networker than a professional tracking down an employment opportunity.

Worse, if you have "the gift of gab," you might run the risk of coming across as "salesy." I see this often. And it can be irritating. Instead, learn to run a structured meeting, and present yourself and speak like the competent professional you intend to be.

— MYTH —

"Networking Is Cheating."

In the professional world, networking meetings, even if not well executed, are common. It's not cheating to these folks. It's all about business. Business is all about relationship-building, and as you're learning here, so is networking. You can be sure that networking is not cheating, and that people won't think *you're* cheating, either.

Here's a different perspective on how it works. In the armed services, one must earn rank and responsibility. That's to say, step-by-step. There are no real shortcuts. You get promoted when you get promoted, if there is an opportunity there.

Well, the professional world works the same—you get promoted when you get promoted, if there is an opportunity there. But there are always, and frequently exceptions. Like getting recruited into something else. Or discovering the same work you're doing, with better pay. Now you have choices. Do you act?

What this means is that there is no single path to any one destination. And because you can get there from anywhere, with any methodology, you can quickly and easily capture professional skills and experiences outside a conventional promotional timeline.

In other words, you're jumping on opportunity. And looking at it this way, you should also see how you can *create* opportunity for yourself—by actively networking.

So cheating really doesn't have anything to do with anything.

It's what and who you *know*; who you *meet*; what you *learn*; and what you *do* with all that information that makes up networking success.

So let this go. Networking is not cheating. It's best business practice.

"No One Wants to Hear Me Talk About Myself."

Actually, people *need* to hear you talk about yourself. And clearly.

Another common positive characteristic among veterans is that things shouldn't be about oneself, but about the group. It's a wonderful attitude, and is part of the serve-others-before-self mentality that comes with service experience. But don't confuse talking about yourself with bragging.

From a professional perspective, clearly explaining your abilities and experience is the difference between you and someone as qualified—even less qualified—getting the job over you. What's right about that? Nothing. Yet it happens. Don't let it happen to you.

So yes, networkers, recruiters and hiring professionals *do* want to hear about you. They just want it to be clear, and easy to understand. Rid this mentality. You're not bragging about your experience. You're stating the facts.

"No One Wants To Meet With a Veteran or Inexperienced Worker"

Au contraire! In fact, many professionals *will* meet with veterans and inexperienced workers. While it's understandable to believe that busy contacts have little time or desire to meet with new or inexperienced jobseekers, running a clean, polished meeting is what makes the difference. Keeping it at 20 minutes is perfect, and is something most busy professionals can handle.

Additionally, those same people know what it's like to enter a job market, too. Most will respect your proactive approach, not to mention that you've kept the meeting brief and structured. After all, a well-prepped, well put-together professional is what *any* job market is looking for.

"The Longer The Meeting, The Better."

This is a common misconception in the professional world. The misconception is that a longer meeting reflects a better or deeper connection with that contact, which in turn would, hopefully, bear more fruit somehow. Sometimes this is true. But most times, it's not. Why? Because long meetings are what keep people from networking in the first place.

A networking meeting is a chance to make a positive connection. Taking an excessive amount of a contact's time appears inconsiderate, and reveals that you don't know how to run a crisp, *mutually* beneficial networking meeting. (Which harks back to my observation that so many networking meetings are ineffective because they're not well-planned or well-run.) That's a lot of counts against you. Keep things brief.

Listening is learning, and networking is give-and-take.
Don't be tempted to talk all about yourself
or what you're in need of.

— MYTH —

"A Networking Meeting Is When I Give A Detailed Description Of My Background."

This myth overlaps with "The Longer the Meeting, the Better." But they are different. While an overview of your military experience, professional experience, education, and qualifications is an essential part of your networking meetings, too much information is not welcome. Not if it isn't asked for. You're there to *learn* as much as you're there to network.

This point is important. You see, your networking contacts are probably not hiring managers. While you will eventually meet those people, your other contacts will think about jobs in fairly general buckets. Electrician. Computer Systems. Auditor. Manager. Operations. Computer Systems. Transportation. Lab Tech. Mechanic. They need to know just enough about your background to connect you with an opportunity if one pops into mind when they are reminded of something relevant. More than that makes things confusing and less memorable. Why? It's simply too difficult to keep track of so much information, especially if the purpose of the meeting is general networking.

"Off The Cuff Is Best; I'll Figure Out Each Meeting When I Get There."

What service member goes into any situation unprepared? Why would a networking meeting be any different? Especially a meeting that could lead to a job?

Remember, this is *employment* we're talking about. If employment is an important factor in your life at all, you can understand the importance of prep here. Besides, weren't you always able to tell when someone showed up unready or underprepared?

From a recruiting and hiring standpoint, it is *immediately* apparent when someone has not prepared for a networking meeting. An executive in transition (looking for a job) came in for such a meeting with me once, sat down, and took off talking in all directions—how talented her peers felt she was, how skilled she was at change management, how strategic her vision was for her industry. I sat across from her and wondered how any of it was relevant to *me*, her networking contact. Now, don't get me wrong—I appreciate spontaneity as much as the next person, but start with something *structured*. An agenda or quick overview of what you'd like to discuss, for instance, would be fabulous. It's helpful to know what we will be talking about.

‹‹‹

An unprepared agenda will have undesired consequences.
Always be prepared for your meetings.

‹‹‹

"People I Know Will Find Me A Job!"

If you are someone who already maintains contacts in the civilian workforce—congratulations, you're on top of one of the most challenging steps in networking. That said, as you network for a job, try to keep in mind that most of your contacts are probably fulfilling their own job responsibilities, and that more often than not, those responsibilities are not recruiting/hiring responsibilities.

Also accept the fact that virtually none of your networking meetings will *immediately* lead to a current opportunity—and remind yourself that this—or asking for job—is not the point to networking anyway. It's about *ultimate*, not immediate, gratification. You simply want to get the "lay of the land." Bringing yourself up to date on what's happening in your future industry is a good goal, for example, as is finding out who's out there, and who might be looking for you.

Think of it this way: If a friend of a friend called *you* right now to request a networking meeting, would you know of an immediate job opening for that person? Would you be prepared to help a banker? A college professor? A machine operator in the packaging industry? Not likely. But when you *do* hear of an opening, you'll probably remember the new friend who requested a 20-minute networking meeting with you, right? Of course you will. And that person will remember you, too.

On recruiters and hiring managers: The same applies when you connect with us. The likelihood that any recruiter will have an open assignment that fits your background is fairly small, *unless* they are recruiting for your background, specifically. Job-fulfillment is nearly always dictated by the needs of the company or our clients. And often, we don't even know what job we'll be filling next. So how could we plug you into something we don't even know exists at the moment?

◇◇

Your contacts are not recruiters or hiring managers.
Never expect a single networking meeting to lead to a
job. Patience is the name of the game.

◇◇

Now that we've debunked some of the myths that surround networking, we'll focus on the hurdle that keeps jobseekers from taking that first step. Let's start with a Real-World Perspective.

Real-World Perspective
("So You Want Me to Go Out There and Grovel, Huh?")

I got a call from a company leader who happened to know my cousin. This very experienced individual, a senior vice president of supply chain, responsible for company-wide management of inventory levels, has an extensive background and pretty impressive accreditation. His job search, however, was at a standstill.

"How's the networking going?" I asked.

"It's nearly impossible getting responses from online applications," he expressed in frustration.

I let him know that online postings were rarely effective for job-search (for the reasons you now know) and assured him that he had a right to feel this way. Then I asked my question again.

"How is the networking going?"

Happy to have another opportunity to vent, he expressed the difficulties of getting through to recruiters and hiring managers, too. I smiled at this—it IS a common gripe—and took the opportunity to explain that by nature of the industry we aren't outplacement counselors (who give job-search guidance), nor do we exist to find jobs for jobseekers. Rather, hiring and recruiting professionals do work for their *clients* (whether that means a single business unit or an entire organization) much like any other business would; it just happens that our commodity of trade is employees instead of, say, products or goods. I had to ask again.

"So, how is the *networking* going?"

It was as though he already knew the truth. He sighed and bottom-lined his answer.

"So you want me to go out there and grovel, huh?"

If I could only tell you how often I have heard this. Not just the tone of voice, but the mentality. No, it is not easy to ask for help. But it's not groveling, either.

No one is going to put opportunity in your lap, no matter who you are, and there are no shortcuts. You must take control of your own circumstances by learning to call on the advice and knowledge of others. To do so is to control the direction of your job search, if not your career.

Now let's take a closer look at why this jobseeker felt so discouraged by the thought of getting out there and networking.

What Makes Networking So Difficult?

(Or: Okay, Okay, I'll Do It.
But It's So Hard!)

Yes, networking is hard work. But you're not alone. Most people are hesitant to network, and when the purpose is to find a new job, they're even more reluctant. And I'm referring to experienced professionals here, who hold one-on-one meetings *every day!*

Let's discuss this.

Maybe you don't like the idea of networking because you feel like you're intruding. Maybe you feel like your request for time is an unwelcome detour into someone's day. Maybe you just don't feel like people want to sit with a stranger. Or maybe you just feel like networking is self-serving.

Very understandable. Really. Because your feelings are probably *right*. (I told you I was going to give you the perspective from the other side of the desk!) And there are reasons—a couple that were addressed at the very beginning of this book: too many networking meetings are too long and too unfocused; and many people are focused solely on themselves. This simply doesn't honor the busy schedule of other people, and makes networking more daunting for the networker as a result.

Remember that every person who agrees to a networking meeting is giving you a *gift* of time. Think of it this way. If your contact happens to work fifty hours per week, your meeting just made it a fifty-one-hour week. That extra hour is because of *your* meeting! That translates to less friend time, less family time, less time for other pursuits, or even for sleep!

Here's one more way to look at it. If your contact is a consultant that charges $200 per hour—say like a lawyer or another kind of service professional, a one-hour networking meeting with you just cost them $200 in billable hours (or at the very least, an hour of selling time). How often do *you* give a gift worth $200?

Probably not too often

◇◇

The time someone gives you is a gift. What does an hour
mean to *you*? Is it worth $200 in billable hours? How
often do *you* give a $200 gift?

◇◇

Ultimately, such long, inconsiderate meetings are what give networking a bad name and why people avoid it. To compound this fear of networking, many are intimidated by the concept of it, too. People tend to envision an hour-long meeting, during which they need to be:

1. socially adept;
2. professionally impeccable; and

3. capable of the above without the need of an agenda.

If that were the case, you'd have to be a corporate and social genius armed with wit and improv skills, right? Well, no wonder you would be hesitant to network. Good thing that's not what we're talking about here.

Making Excuses

So what *am* I talking about? I'm talking about making contact, conducting *brief* meetings, and following up. *That's it.* It's something that, in many ways, you've likely been doing all this time, even in the service—just without process or practice. Of course, the circumstances of networking are a bit different, but you can't let that get in your way. Yes, it's tough not to feel embarrassed or unsure about networking, especially when entering a strange professional world from your last professional world. But it should *never* be a reason to avoid networking.

Over the years, I've witnessed professionals—including company leaders—busy themselves with all sorts of "job-seeking activities" to procrastinate or avoid networking for a job, all because of the feeling of embarrassment, shyness, or apprehension. You probably know or have heard these kinds of excuses, too—like tweaking and re-tweaking your resume, perpetually checking emails or online job posts, or even constant research or "prep" for a (hopeful) job interview. It's hard to imagine, but I've even known executives who have shopped for the right outfit or shoes that are "a must" before getting an interview! I assure you—I've heard them all.

So, what do you *do* to get rid of these fears and embarrassments? Commit yourself to learning how to conduct a *structured* networking meeting and remind yourself that no matter how well or poorly a meeting may go, you're already doing *much* more for your job search than even some of the most experienced civilian professionals out there.

Three Real Perspectives on Networking

The idea of networking hits all of us differently. The following examples highlight three different networking perspectives. I chose composite examples based on what I hear all the time. Here's what a few had to say, followed by my reactions.

Kolby

Kolby found a construction job right out of the Army. At first he was grateful to gain employment when so many of his buddies couldn't even land interviews. And though the Army made him easily qualified for the work, Kolby came to realize it wasn't the kind of job he wanted for the long run and that he wasn't using a lot of his Army skills. Plus, the pay wasn't good, and the hours were long. As a result, there had been little time to find other work.

"Now it's a year later, and I feel like I wasted time. I don't know anybody outside of the construction industry, and I don't have a way with words. I don't know how I'm going meet people for new things, and keep conversations going. And I don't want to feel like a fool."

Don't worry about having wasted time. Time is never wasted if you do something with the information you've gained along the way. Also, don't worry about having a limited network. Many people find themselves starting from the beginning, even in the business world. If you're not a talker, and tight on time, you'll do great with the model of The 20-Minute Networking Meeting. *It's designed to help you construct and lead a brief, but informative discussion.*

MY SUGGESTION:

Sometimes professionals feel that, despite their accomplishments inside their organizations, they have not taken the time to build networks outside their organizations or circumstances. If you have family members or friends outside your professional circle, they are a start. So is your neighborhood. So is your faith community or civic group. Former shipmates, team, staff, airmen, buddies, and colleagues are all great contacts. You probably have a much broader network than you realize, if you just consider who you already know.

Libby

Libby gained a lot of programming experience in the Air Force that hadn't reached the civilian world yet. Aware of this and wanting a head start, she started hitting the civilian job boards before leaving the service.

"It's just faster," she says. "I know how to use all the boards and databases better than most people, which gives me an edge."

However, in spite of applying for dozens of things in all corners of the country, Libby's search did not turn up prospects before she was discharged. She returned home.

While Libby's people skills are satisfactory, she's also shy. And due to her affinity for technology, her primary job-searching method has been kept to web-surfing. "I still have a farther reach than what's near me. I think I can find a job over the net without getting help from people."

WHAT I SAID:

You can't really conduct an effective job search in a vacuum. People *hire people—not our technology—and making personal connections is going to be key to your job search. Don't spend all your time on the web. While the Internet might give you a longer geographic reach, many hiring managers will not spend time recruiting professionals who don't already live in their market anyway. Also try to remember that nearly everyone has a way to access the net these days; whether you're better on a computer or not, it means significantly more competition. In the end, it will be* networking *that tells you what you need to know about your specific job market. And it will be* direct contact *with those people that gets you in front of other decision-makers.*

MY SUGGESTION:

Try to limit online postings to only 20-30% of your available job-search time. Use the rest of your availability to pick up the phone, send emails, or have lunch with those who can help you make your next connection.

Joss

Joss has been out of the Navy for three years. She has avoided networking, and has taken odd jobs to pay the bills until something better comes along. But after three years of searching and waiting, nothing. Networking, she has now realized, is the only sure path to landing employment.

"My job-search coach wants me to start networking with

people I used to associate with through a chamber of commerce group. The truth is, I don't really know them very well. And to call people I barely know and ask for time in the middle of their workday doesn't seem right. I know how many hours a week these people work. And some travel a lot. How many of them are going to want to take time to meet with me?"

WHAT I SAID:

You're right about several things. Yes, you'll be contacting people you don't know well. And no, not all of them will have time to meet with you. That's part of the nature of networking. I'm afraid that you'll just have to forge ahead with the caveats you've expressed. But start with the people you know best. Think about the people you talk to most. Perhaps there are even former Navy colleagues you know well, or have "gone the extra mile for" over the years. They have a perspective on this stuff, too. Just begin networking with people you are comfortable with and who will likely be receptive to your call.

MY SUGGESTION:

Try to remember that networking is about give-and-take. Include how you can help others versus how others can help you. This is a difference-maker, and will help you feel like you're a partner and not a bother to the people you contact.

When you're ready, spend extra time on Key Question 5, about giving back to the people you meet with. (This can be found in the Great Discussion chapter.) Don't lose that sense of gratitude! It goes a long way with someone who puts a busy schedule on hold to meet with you.

OVERALL

Try to remember that networking is not about being slick and smooth. It's about developing relationships through brief, meaningful interactions over the course of time. As relationship-building *takes* time, doing this now helps you avoid networking problems down the road.

Now for the Good Stuff

So far, we've discussed what networking is and why it works, and we've talked about a number of myths that surround networking for veteran jobseekers. We've also seen some examples of veterans struggling with the idea of incorporating networking into their job searches. Take some time to think about your own experience, and try to identify ways some of these misperceptions have affected your search so far. But come back soon, because we're about to begin a crash course in conducting the best networking meetings possible.

Now's the time for a quick coffee break.

Ready?
Let's do it!

PART II

The 20-Minute Networking Meeting

Objectives & Strategy

You made it! We'll keep this short and get right to it. By the way—if you have not read the first part of this book, don't skip it. Part II will make more sense with the context provided by Part I. Besides, as a veteran you know that a tried and true process works if you just do your part. Setting the foundation for these networking learnings now is setting yourself up for networking success in the future.

YOUR OBJECTIVE IN JOB NETWORKING

Okay, so you're looking for work. Your overall mission is to land a new, terrific job, right? Sure. But what if your new networking contacts wouldn't know of open positions in the first place? Then these are your objectives in networking:

- Gather new information
- Add new contacts to your list
- Gain an evangelist

Now let's take a closer look at each of these objectives and how they will help you achieve your *20MNM* goals.

Gather New Information

WHAT IT MEANS: Listening. Questioning. Absorbing (and *writing down*) what is said to you.

THE REASON: Networking is a way to learn from contacts firsthand. It's also a chance to share what you know with your contacts to get reactions and redirection. It's quite an opportunity. You'll be giving as much as you're receiving!

You always want a *modest* goal for gathering information from any one networking meeting. Every person will have a few nuggets of value for you. Examples would be:

- Informs you on your current qualifications in your future functional area
- Helps you assess your service skills for civilian application
- Helps you translate your service skills into civilian industry terms
- Helps you transition into the civilian work environment
- Informs how/where you fit into certain or chosen companies or industries
- Helps you determine who may be hiring

VERY IMPORTANT:

Don't expect more than a few nuggets from each contact!

Remember, this is a brief *meeting*, not a seminar.

Add New Contacts to Your List

WHAT IT MEANS: Getting additional names. These could be:

- Veterans that got out of the service before you
- Other people in your and your contacts' industries or future function
- People in your target companies or industries
- *Anyone* else who could help in your job search

THE REASON: Contacts—especially the way we're defining the term here—are people who know you. Period. As it pertains to job search, they are simply people who are somehow connected to your line of work, industry, or other industries and professions. Keep in mind: the more people who know you, the more information there is *about you* in the marketplace. The more your name is circulating in that marketplace, the more likely you will be connected to a great new opportunity.

WHY YOU WOULD DO IT: Because while you're out there trying to find a job, employers are out there trying to find you! You want to have a presence in the Invisible Job Market for exactly this reason. If you don't, you'll be left in the dark. Do you recall that 70-80% of all jobs are obtained through the people you know? And do you recall our scenario where Passive Candidate ended up in the glow of his computer while Active Candidate inserted herself into the radar of the working world? It all happens by adding new people to your network.

VERY IMPORTANT:

While there are exceptions, most jobseekers land their next job not from their own *original* list of networking contacts, or even from the contacts gained from that original group, but through the "third ring" of people (i.e., friends of friends of friends). It's only through active networking that you'll get to the third ring.

Gain an Evangelist

WHAT IT MEANS: A jobseeker needs an evangelist, which is someone willing to take positive action on their behalf. More than an advocate, an evangelist is like your own personal ambassador. These people will have a *major impact* on your networking. Developing one is something you must try to do with each new networking meeting by way of excellent prep and presentation.

THE REASON: Once you've got an evangelist on your side, you're on your way to twice the pay-off, but half the work. Here's what an evangelist might do for you:

- Forward your resume
- Recommend you to someone who is hiring
- Check his or her company's internal postings to see if anything is a fit for you
- Contact you later with additional ideas
- Introduce you to someone else
- Suggest you for a project

WHY YOU WOULD DO IT: Why *wouldn't* you do it? Having someone who sings your praises, recommends you to personal contacts, and thinks of you first in a job search? Hmm. Not a lot to expand on here.

Now, despite what you may think, *developing* this kind of contact is very simple. If you've ever bought a beer or brought lunch to someone while in the service, and that gesture came back to you in the same or different way, then you know the value of an evangelist. They are people who look out for you.

(Now imagine if you had a network of them.)

Military or no, for most of us it's in our nature to help others (though the desire wanes if our time is wasted). And most people in a position to help you likely got there because someone helped *them* first.

HOW YOU WOULD DO IT: Think about meeting new professional contacts. As you meet with those people, you will be there to learn and observe two things:

1. Their skills and abilities as related to what they do for a living.
2. How they act in a professional setting (we'll expand on that more in a second).

Now let's turn the focus to you. You'll be giving the same clear impression of how *you* act in a professional setting, and you'll also leave an impression of what *you* have to offer the working world.

When these things line up and that new contact becomes convinced by your background and experience (not by selling or persuading) that you fit within their network somewhere, that person may become an evangelist.

Make sense? Let's put it in simpler terms, just for clarity's sake: When people really like you and have an appreciation for your work history and experience (even if it's limited!), they will likely want to go to bat for you. Especially if they sincerely believe your talent and offering should have a place somewhere in the working universe. Why would someone do that? Well, aside from wanting to help another person—you—it's because having you in *their* network benefits them, too. How? Because if *they* develop a relationship with *you*, then you become a potential: client; customer; a person who would refer business; friend; expert; or valued networking contact, for any reason not listed here.

Remember, we *all* need each other.

In the long run, when you're eventually in a position to give back in a professional, or even personal context (including their own possible future job search), it's a relationship that already has a foundation and history.

Looking at it this way, the opportunity to give back or serve others is always present.

It is crucial to keep in mind, however, that most of the time the people you are networking with *are not interviewing you for a job*. They will not be in a position to evaluate your skill set (because they're not hiring managers), nor will they evaluate your abilities and background against a particular hiring situation (because they're not interviewing you).

On the other hand, it *is* important that you don't treat a networking meeting as just a social interaction or a chance to make a new friend. Those things are fine, but your main objective in networking is to make a solid, positive impression about how you act in a professional setting.

Assuming that you are meeting a networking contact for the first time, or reconnecting with someone you don't know well, you want to leave an impression that will prompt that person to recommend or refer you to others. Think about professionals that you most admire (e.g. other veterans or officers; business leaders you've met or know about; leaders in your industry, and so on). As you narrow them down, ask yourself: what characteristics do I admire about them?

Now think about your *own* positive professional characteristics. Do a few come to mind? Now is the time to show them. Here's what you want to come across in each networking meeting:

- You are positive (*upbeat tone, language, overall positivity*)
- You are strategic (*you know why you are there*)
- You are well organized (*by managing your meeting well, keeping a close tab on topics and time*)
- You are gracious (*appreciative and grateful for the time that was spent with you*)
- You follow through after a meeting (*prompt follow-up, meaningful ongoing interactions*)

Does this sound like someone you would recommend for a job or refer to a colleague? It does to me!

You've probably heard the phrase "It's not *what* you know, it's *who* you know," when it comes to networking. While that is certainly true, there is a related sentiment that is equally true. "There's no second chance at a first impression." Leave 'em impressed!

Who You Are
(Or: Who You're *Supposed* to Be)

We've discussed your contacts and even touched on the angelic offerings of a potential evangelist. Before we get too far, however, have you thought about what type of professional *you* aspire to be? In *addition* to what you have learned in the service, are you someone who is well organized? Proactive? Accountable? Do you manage projects and time effectively? Do you set and achieve objectives? Do others like being around you? Are you gracious to others? Do you redirect and follow up again if need be?

The demands are certainly a tall order to fill, but if you've witnessed the achievements of a successful career, whether in or out of the service, then you understand that these are common characteristics. And now is the time to exhibit them yourself. Why? Because in a networking meeting, you want to showcase your professional attitude as much as—if not more than—you want to carefully explain your skills and abilities. It's a big part of that overall impression. After all, would you hire someone with great skills and poor interpersonal style? No, probably not. So would you expect your networking contacts to feel any different? No, probably not.

◇◇

CHARACTERISTICS YOU WANT TO EXHIBIT DURING YOUR NETWORKING MEETINGS:
Positivity
Strategic abilities
Impressive planning and organization skills
Strong communication skills
Generosity and gratitude
Follow-through

◇◇

Since we're on the topic of professional integrity, here's a great example of reputation and the power of evangelism. I call it:

"Everybody Loves This Woman!"

A few years back, I conducted a search for the top leader in a nationally known literary organization. I made over 100 calls around the country to potential candidates and sources. One of the first people I called recommended a woman located in New York City. We'll call her Sarah Brown. I already had Sarah Brown in my database as someone to call, because she was fairly visible in the industry. But I noted the recommendation anyway. It's important to keep track of these things.

Imagine my surprise when another person I called also suggested Sarah Brown. Then another. And another.

In the end, seven people suggested that I call Sarah Brown about this job. Seven.

Eventually, Sarah and I talked about the opportunity I was recruiting for. We discussed her background, interests, credentials, and also what was required of this new role. Ultimately, it was not a fit for either side. But with such an army of evangelists behind her, it's hard to avoid thinking of Sarah when other opportunities come up. It's quite a powerful position to be in as a professional. People are doing work for her, and quite often, Sarah doesn't even know it. Wouldn't you like to experience the same?

I'm happy to report that Sarah landed a great new position shortly after our discussion. She's now head of one of the largest and most respected literary organizations in world. My guess is that she'll never be without a leadership opportunity in her career again. She's the kind of evangelist-making professional *every* job-seeker should aspire to be.

The 20-Minute Networking Meeting

What It Is and Where It Came From

The question we're most asked is "Can one really cover enough ground in 20 minutes?" The answer is a resounding *Yes*, and we'll show you exactly how. For the moment, allow me to explain how the material was culled from the experiences of others and actuated by a presentation I attended.

I was invited to a business event that featured a local speaker and a topic I was interested in. Oftentimes, such presentations can be long, depending on the speaker, the size of the group, the material and so on. (You have probably had the same experience in the service.) So I showed up prepared for a long Power Point. But I was in for a real surprise.

Just as the speaker seemed to get rolling...he finished. I remember wondering if I was late. But everyone else seemed as surprised as I was (by the way we were all looking at one another), and the group eventually got out of their seats. We were actually *done!*

And that's when it hit me. The speaker's brevity wasn't just a welcome change to his presentation-going audience, but actually a slick strategy that brought sharp focus to his topic and made *effective use* of everyone's time. It was almost laughable in its effect. *People stuck around.* With extra time and the author's book on our hands, we were now free to be a self-engaged audience to come or go as we pleased. Many began asking meaningful questions about his material. And why wouldn't we? That was the whole reason we were there in the first place!

In retrospect, the speaker's outcome was even *better* than what I observed at the time. So much so that I'm now relating the story of his book and presentation to you.

Now *that's* impact.

After leaving the event, I took some time to understand exactly what the speaker did to pull off such a feat. Here's what happened in all its simplistic glory. Somewhere after introducing his book (which he gave to all the attendees), the author threw out some juicy bits about its contents, pulled us in *juuust* enough to capture our interest, and then cut us free. From there, with no pressure to stay or involve ourselves, the audience actually engaged, and *that was that.* It couldn't have been more perfect. Or short!

In the business world, such presentations and workshops can be important to your overall professional development. But after a time, it can sometimes feel like such classes are going to be too long, too detailed, or too irrelevant. Consequently, we sometimes want to go, and sometimes we *have* to.

Well, networking meetings can be the same in many ways. Occasionally people *want* to do them, and sometimes, they feel that they *have* to. Oftentimes, like a presentation, the meeting becomes too long, and if it's ill-planned or lacking in focus, it holds the *contact* captive, a waste of his or her time.

I contemplated this while considering the hundreds of networking meetings I had banked in the last few years and asked myself, "What *is* too long? What is too short? Is there a happy medium?"

As I slowly pulled this information together, I also *really* began to pay attention to the clock during meetings. I observed, more often than not, that people were pushing hour-long networking meetings—whether they had requested that much time or not. And once I came to *that* realization, I decided there had to be a better way.

My conclusion, as you know by now, was that an hour is *a lot* for what actually needs to be discussed in a networking meeting. I began observing what an hour of networking time was taking away from me (work, which backed up; family time, which you can never get back; social time with friends; and, for goodness' sake, *sleep*). It was all adding up to a lot of *life*. Heck, there are barely enough hours in the day for *work!*

So next, I began to distill. I gathered the best approaches that the best networkers brought to the table and kept close track of the weakest methodologies. And of course, I did this while keeping track of time. This is what I found:

A full hour (even for an executive recruiter who is accustomed to this) *lost my attention*. Right around the thirty-minute mark, I started to consider what else I had to accomplish that day. Distraction set in as I began to stress about the work piling up behind me.

Thirty minutes was better than an hour and, yes, I was less distracted, but it's still the length of a full TV sitcom (with commercials!). And the mutual benefit was still too small. Where was the vital information about the networker? And why hadn't we hit those points in thirty full minutes?

Fifteen minutes was much better. Remembering the aforementioned speaker's short presentation, I focused on what my shorter meetings looked like. These weren't traditional networking meetings, but rather networkers dropping by or asking to just stop in and shake hands in the lobby. Fifteen minutes wasn't enough to learn about the people I was speaking with, and some of those precious minutes were being taken up by required hellos and proper goodbyes. And then I found the "happy medium."

Twenty minutes, as it turns out, is exactly the right amount of time to warm into a conversation, get a good sense of someone's background and goals, and see the person off properly. Over the course of time, this seemed to prove itself true time and time again.

Not wanting it to be just my opinion, I shared the idea with my business partners and a few other networkers. Universally, they concluded that this observation was spot-on. When the meetings were shorter they were better! Bingo!

After bringing the finer points of networking together (mind you, this is *years'* worth of networking) and collecting the experiences of a number of colleagues, a perfect, twenty-minute package of give-and-take networking emerged. Ultimately, it was structured into *The 20-Minute Networking Meeting*. Which brings us to the book you're holding now.

The 20-Minute Networking Meeting is the distillation of decades of concepts. With the express goal of making each networking meeting do the most it can for you, it is specifically built for your job search as a veteran, and designed to meet the needs of both you and your networking contacts.

Back to it. Here are the golden rules to remember:

- Each part is **important** and has a **purpose**
- There are **five steps** and **five questions**
- You should **follow them** *exactly* so that you get a command of the process

NOTE: As you become familiar with the *20MNM* format, you *can* allow yourself flexibility by tweaking your timing and agenda. Networking is a people activity. Conversations take turns and jump off topic. This is okay, so long as you use professional discretion to get back on track when you're too far off agenda. Again, you won't always have to stick to 20 minutes. But 'til then, follow the steps 'til you know it well!

What To Do First

Before you hit the job market and start networking, you've got to be ready. Really ready. Do not begin networking (and certainly do not begin interviewing for jobs) until you're prepared.

How?

There are a lot of ways to be prepared to hit the job market—having an updated resume and a prepared "elevator speech" (explaining yourself and/or background in a relatively short amount of time); planning your networking activities; and identifying target companies or organizations you are interested in, among others. But the most important readiness factor before beginning the job search is your psychological state.

Psychological state? Yes, your psychological state.

This might be a delicate topic for some, but I have found that the vast majority of challenges to jobseekers are issues relating to their psychological state. For nearly anyone, being in job transition is painful. Whether you're a civilian looking for a job, or a veteran getting back into civilian life, job search can sometimes can get *real* tough with unexpected challenges down the road. *But*...this is okay. Really. After all, if you have freshly separated from the service, you're probably still used to its rhythms, people, processes, and day-to-day life. Of *course* it's going to be abrupt and challenging when you transition. Civilians experience the same thing. They leave all the people, processes, and day-to-day work they've known for years, to begin something that is unknown to them, with people they do not know.

Yes, transition is often (and understandably) upsetting.

But this upset takes a toll and can sabotage your networking and job search efforts. (Civilian or veteran.) A sad, panicked or depressed state is not a ready state. Again, the emotional roller coaster of life is okay and natural. And taking time to deal with it is not only acceptable, but critical. If you find that you are fearful or panicked about not finding a job (or if you have no feelings about the situation at all), it's simply too soon to begin networking. You could jump into things anyway, but mark my words when I say that it will have adverse effects on your meetings. Mental readiness is key. Here's such a scenario.

Last year, Phillip, a former Navy officer, was looking for new work. Reflecting back on the early months of his unemployment, he realized that he had felt and acted rude in some networking situations. "Some people weren't particularly helpful or follow up with information, like names or job leads, and I got frustrated," he explained. But after getting critical feedback from a fellow veteran already in the workforce, he came to realize that he had been treating his meetings as though he were still in the service. His behavior and attitude were more at home in the service, but it was received differently in civilian contexts. Respected for getting things done in the Navy, Phillip realized he was coming off as edgy at times. His networking meetings and introductions had virtually stopped as a result.

"I feel like I burned bridges with those earlier meetings," he said. Unfortunately, he's probably right.

Why make that same mistake if you can see it coming?

In a business case, there was my meeting with Jane, a job-seeking executive. Jane's manner of speaking was curt, her voice extra loud, and her gestures unusually expansive. She spoke at length about the faults of her prior employer. When I asked if perhaps she was struggling a bit with the change in her employment status, she slammed her hand on the desk. I literally jumped. Her voice was angry and the volume was high. "NO!" she yelled. She was actually shaking. I moved on to another topic, but concluded that any referrals to other networking contacts would be embarrassing for me and fruitless for her.

Now contrast Jane and Phillip with Bob, a U.S. Army Corps of Engineers leader who was *very* comfortable with his transition. Helping me understand how his unusual service background was already incorporated into the civilian workforce, he approached our discussion in a straightforward, positive manner. He made no criticisms; there was no negativity in what he had to say of his experiences or circumstances; and he was forward-thinking as a networker. Not just that, but he accomplished his meeting inside of 20 minutes.

We had a great discussion. We laughed a lot, and I was ultimately was able to offer Bob some job search tips and advice, while he told me more about USACE operations, which informed material in this book. A win-win for both of us!

BOTTOM LINE: Take time for yourself. It's important. Whether you are recently out of the service or a seasoned professional rejoining the workforce, it takes *time* to get mentally ready.

As a closing thought, it's worth mentioning that in the service, you probably developed the (healthy) habit of *"getting the job done"* in quick, efficient fashion. This characteristic is deeply appreciated in and *by* all professionals, and it comes in spades with you as a veteran. Really—you have an edge here. But I don't need to tell you that a rushed job is not a good job. That a weak foundation will not hold up the house, and that if it tumbles down, will be damaging if not catastrophic to your momentum and self-confidence. Which is your foundation. I also don't need to tell you that it's impossible to be a confident networker when you're lacking confidence in yourself as a jobseeker. *Be ready.*

Turn to page 143 for a quick exercise that will help you assess your own readiness to get into the job market. Once you've spent some time with these questions and feel confident in your answers, come back as we dive into the framework of *The 20-Minute Networking Meeting.*

Your 20-Minute Networking Meeting Cheat Sheet

All right, now we're rollin'. Here's a very brief overview of what's coming. Another Cheat Sheet will be available again at the end of the book for easy, usable reference. (See page 142.) Note the time frames for each step. *The 20-Minute Networking Meeting* is really this simple. It consists of five parts:

STEP 1:	**Great First Impression**	2–3 minutes
STEP 2:	**Great Veteran Overview**	1 minute
STEP 3:	**Great Discussion**	12–15 minutes
STEP 4:	**Great Ending**	2 minutes
STEP 5:	**Great Follow-Up**	After the Meeting

And that's it!

Each one of these steps will be detailed in the pages to come, letting you know what to do, how to do it, and why.

FIRST UP: STEP 1 — Great First Impression

Step 1—
Great First Impression

GOAL:	To make a great first impression
HOW:	With thanks and short chitchat
TIME LIMIT:	2 to 3 minutes
WHAT YOU WILL DO:	Arrive, express gratitude, highlight connections, set the agenda
NOTE:	Turn to page 148 for your Great First Impression Planner

ARRIVING FOR YOUR 20-MINUTE NETWORKING MEETING

Arrive a few minutes early. If you're meeting at a coffee shop or restaurant, arrive as early as you'd like. If you're meeting at your contact's place of business (I'm speaking from experience here), don't arrive too early.

THE REASON: If you're meeting at a public place, you can do as you please. But if you're meeting at your contact's workplace, it can be uncomfortable for them to know that someone is waiting—especially if he or she has work to do before the meeting. In the past, I've had guests arrive up to forty-five minutes early. It's not my habit to keep guests waiting, but giving up lunch or a much needed break to start a meeting way ahead of the scheduled time isn't exactly something most people care to do either. It can result in a meeting with a distracted or annoyed contact. And if the point to networking is obtaining information, you don't want an annoyed or distracted contact.

WHAT TO DO: If you find yourself with extra time, find a place to sit and work outside the office. Review your notes for your meeting. Take a stroll around the block to collect your thoughts. Maybe you'll even see something interesting to talk about in your meeting.

Here are some other things to concern yourself with until your appointment:

- Double check: Do you have your resume, pen, and notebook?
- Are you prepared for the questions and topics that you wish to discuss?
- If you're in the office, take a look around. What do your surroundings tell you about this organization and its culture?

◇◇

TIP:

Familiarizing yourself with your environment will help
you feel more comfortable before your networking
meeting. It may even provide some informal conversation
as you begin your discussion. Take a look around!

◇◇

Don't be fooled. Your first impression starts the moment you arrive for your meeting. Be respectful toward anybody who greets you (assistants, front desk people). This is essential to remember because often your contact will ask their opinion of you. ("Was she friendly? Courteous? Appreciative?")

EXPRESSING GRATITUDE

Before there is any networking discussion, share a hearty smile and a firm (not aggressive) handshake during your introduction. And look your contact in the eye. You'd be surprised how often I get feedback from clients telling me that even executive candidates have inadequate eye contact.

In the professional world, eye contact shows respect and that you are engaged in the conversation. *Lack* of eye contact gives the sense that you may be shy or nervous, which often leaves the impression of inexperience. That would suggest that you're not ready for a networking meeting. And if you're not ready for a meeting, why would you be ready for the professional world?

Once you get a lock on your introduction, express your gratitude. Perhaps you already thanked your contact by email or over the phone when you set up the meeting, but it's always necessary to offer thanks again, now that you're face-to-face.

THE REASON: Remember—this person is giving you the *gift* of time. Acknowledging that fact in an earnest manner will earn you a lot of respect and gratitude in return. As far as how to express your thanks, you can do that any way you'd like. Here are a few examples to start with.

> *"It's great to see you, Lorn. Thank you again for meeting with me."*

> *"Hi, Serena! What a great office! Again, thank you for agreeing to see me."*

> *"Pleasure to meet you, Major Donovan. I really appreciate your time today."*

As you can tell, it doesn't have to be anything too fancy; it's simply the thought that counts.

All right, so now you have a grip on introductions. Next . . .

HIGHLIGHT CONNECTIONS

Though your meeting may start with a little small talk around the artwork in the lobby or the scenery you saw outside, a better way toward a great impression is by highlighting mutual connections.

THE REASON: If you don't know the person you are meeting with all that well, it can be a safe way to bridge the gap. People feel more comfortable knowing that they have acquaintances in common. And there are many ways to make this connection, so don't worry if you don't have a close connection to your contact.

WHAT TO DO:

- Remind the other person of who connected you in the first place:
  "Jessamine Farley asked to send her greetings. Jessamine has been kind enough to introduce me to a few people since getting out of the Marines, and she said you were a

big help to her."

- Mention other people you know in common:
  "I think we might have people in common at Veteran Women Business Owners. Do you know Iris Gussie or Tommie Phebe?"

If it seems you have no one in common (because you connected with someone via email or LinkedIn, for instance), you can try these approaches:

- Suggest other likely professional connections:
  "I saw your LinkedIn profile. I think we both volunteer at Legion #567."

- Ask about a person you both may know (but only if you think it is likely; don't do this just for sake of banter):
  "Are you a member of the Smallville youth hockey league? Do you happen to know Rob Silas? We were in basic together."

Or, if appropriate, you could make a personal connection. (By appropriate, I mean that crossing personal boundaries could come across as creepy and make your contact uncomfortable.)

"I read that you were stationed at Warren Air Force Base near Cheyenne. I thought about the U of Wyoming in Laramie before enlisting."

Or:

"Your website bio mentioned that you live in Platteville. I grew up in nearby LaSalle before heading to the Coast Guard."

TO REPEAT: You should use the last example only if you believe it would be well received. Taking your professional networking meeting into the personal realm can be a powerful tool, but it can backfire easily if your contact does not care to discuss anything other than business.

At this point, you now have your introductions and expression of gratitude behind you. What's next? Getting to the point. (And feel free to state you're doing so!)

SETTING THE AGENDA

Here it is—the moment of (literal) truth. Tell your contact you're only going to take twenty minutes, and share exactly what you're hoping to talk about in that time. That's it.

THE REASON: As you've already read in this book, most people expect a networking meeting to take an hour. Even when someone says, "Really, just a few minutes of your time." However, you can reaffirm your promise of twenty minutes by laying out an actual agenda ahead of the discussion. This will help your contact believe that you'll keep to your promise of twenty minutes.

Here are a few more reasons why setting the agenda is important.

It will set the tone of:

- The meeting
- The impression you create
- Your overall job-search approach

In addition, it will show that you are:

- Prepared
- Considerate of your contact's time
- Unafraid to lead

WHAT TO DO: Introductions and gratitude out of the way, hit the seats and start the meeting by stating your intent, and conveying that you only need a small amount of their time.

REMEMBER: The person is doing you the courtesy of meeting with you. Return the courtesy by acknowledging that fact.

Let's see what a couple of examples would look like (and don't worry—you don't have to get too fancy with this, either):

> *"Thanks again for meeting with me, Kyrsten. I just need twenty minutes. I want to give you a brief overview of my experience and background and ask a few questions that help in my job search."*

> *"This will be brief, Andra. I just hope to mention a few of my military, academic and professional highlights and get your perspective on a few things related to my career research."*

And that's it. Really! If you care to be a little more specific, you can do so. But keep it short and crisp, and stick with the two to three-minutes you have for this step.

REAL-WORLD PERSPECTIVE

Veteran Army Captain Paul successfully used *The 20-Minute Networking Meeting* in his own job search. I asked if following the *20MNM* structure made a difference to his networking, and he said:

"Absolutely. Probably the first key piece of the structure that helped me the most, is to be succinct in the beginning and be clear about what the goal is in the meeting. The one thing that I *am* good at is talking. But it's important to not talk so much, especially during networking meetings or job interviews. *You* want them to know a lot about you, but they don't care about that much information. They want to know what's important to *them*. The structure of the book allowed me to trim it down."

◇◇◇

A VERY IMPORTANT SIDE NOTE:

Though it is important to make your agenda clear, please remember that you *do* have flexibility when you need it. I know I've expressed this notion already, but if your introduction goes well and your chitchat extends past your first two minutes, that's *totally okay!* Just be sensitive—if your chatting goes for five minutes or more, checking with your contact or do your best to get things back on track to not overstay your welcome. The only exception here is if your contact is leading your talk, in which case, check-in. Then follow that lead—but again, stay sensitive.

◇◇◇

ALSO IMPORTANT:

Don't wait for your contact to start the discussion. *You* called the meeting and it is your responsibility to manage it. After all, would you agree to attend a meeting called by somebody else who expects you to run it for them? Probably not. Be the leader that you are, and lead!

REAL-WORLD PERSPECTIVE — WHERE IS THE AGENDA?

A job-seeking executive came in for a meeting and plopped down in the chair across from me once. We exchanged a few pleasantries, and then . . . nothing. No agenda, no plan for the meeting.

Because it was not my responsibility to lead this person's meeting, I let the awkward silence play out, wondering if this executive, previously in a role leading an international company, would catch on and grab hold of his meeting. He did not. A number of explanations went through my mind, but it struck me as strange that a CEO would ask for a meeting and expect me (or some other person) to help, yet run the meeting. It did not leave me with a good impression.

In the end, I found a way to participate in the meeting anyway, and even gave the person a helpful suggestion or two. But I did not offer any networking names. My thought was that if I sent him to any of my contacts, he would conduct himself the same way. My contacts are too important to me, and I could not have them thinking I endorse such behavior. Bound by that fear, I was forced to play it safe, and meted out only minimal assistance. I know by experience that this jobseeker left our meeting with some sense of "success," having networked and gained a couple of tips. But he lost the chance to get some meaningful contacts, and certainly to gain an evangelist.

Why didn't I help him more? Why didn't I take the time to teach him how to conduct a networking meeting?

The answer is simple: It's not a professional service for offer. There are, in fact, outplacement consultants and career coaches who work with jobseekers to help them plan and execute their job search. It's just not part of the work that *I* do.

The people you are networking with are not likely to be professional job coaches and resume writers, either. That is not their job. It is *your* job to have the right resources to help you frame up your job search. And certainly don't expect them to set the agenda for your meeting, either. *You're* in control of the meeting. Take charge!

Step 2 —
Great Veteran Overview

GOAL:	Give a great overview of your service and/or professional background
HOW:	Providing a crisp, brief, and memorable understanding of your work experience
TIME LIMIT:	1 minute (You want to leave time for your Great Discussion!)
WHAT YOU WILL DO:	Briefly state your experience
NOTE:	Turn to page 150 for your One-Minute Overview Planner

BREAKING DOWN YOUR ONE MINUTE

Right about here you're probably reeling over "one minute."

"Whoa, whoa," you say. "How am I going to talk about my professional experience in 60 seconds? Especially when it's all my services terms and acronyms?

Or perhaps you have a limited amount of professional experience to begin with, and are wondering if you have *enough* to talk about in the first place.

Is it really possible to give a full snapshot of yourself in 60 seconds? Even with non-civilian terms and acronyms?

The answer is a resounding *Yes,* and I'll show you exactly how.

For the moment, however, let's establish why a one-minute set up of your background is so crucial to your overall 20-minute discussion.

THE REASON: A one-minute overview is efficient and strategic. The objective is to provide a *general* sense of what you've done, which provides context for your Great Discussion (next chapter). With a clean-as-a-whistle, one-minute snapshot, your contacts can think about who to connect you with or where you "fit" job-wise when they hear of an opening.

REMEMBER: The objective of your networking meeting is to gather information, gain a contact or two, and to create an evangelist. If you find that you have *more* than a minute's worth of material (or, say, a lot of armed services terminology), choose carefully; you want to avoid extra details that may be irrelevant and difficult to understand or remember. It may bog people down for this kind of meeting. (You're networking, not interviewing, remember.) The idea is to keep things to a minimum so that you may discuss the real information you're after.

A special note on armed services jargon. Most civilians won't understand the terminology, ranking system, acronyms and abbreviations that come with your service experience. Consequently, veterans lose out on job opportunities because networkers and interviewers are *unable* to comprehend the full depth and scope of your skills and experience—in spite of how qualified you may be for the job! The takeaway: learning how to translate your service skills is *crucial* to your networking and job search, and is a skill in itself. It's how people will "get" what you (know how to) do, and where you actually fit in their network, company or industry. And there's great news: *all* of your skills are transferable. You just have to help other people understand *how*, through the translating that you learn to do. Because this book is meant to show you how to structure and run a networking meeting, it does not focus on skills translation. It does, however, include how those translations will look and sound, and how to use them during everyday, civilian meetings. Read on.

WHAT TO DO:

- Tally your years in your particular job function, and/or in the armed services
- Highlight your background (civilian and/or service)
- Add where you've worked (civilian and/or service)
- String them all together

Here they are again, with examples. (Fully written overviews will follow.)

Think number of years in the function:

"For eight years, I was an Army Non-Commissioned Officer (NCO), similar to a company Manager or Director."

"I was a Cyber Operations Specialist for four years in the Navy, and have been a small business IT Security Lead the last three."

Consider the highlights of your background:

"I received Marines training and education as a Non-Commissioned Officer."

"I oversaw a squad of twelve people, responsible for a million dollar budget and supplies."

Followed by places you've worked:

"I spent two years active duty in the Air Force, and two in

the reserves."

"*Before four years in the Coast Guard, District 9, I worked at GrayCo for two.*"

<hr>

TIP:

Need a kick-start to your recalling your services experiences? Obtain or review a copy of your discharge papers. (DD-214 Form; Certificate of Release; Discharge from Active Duty, among other names. Dig in!)

<hr>

Getting a feel for it? Here are three more examples of the high-level view of information you want to share regarding your specific experiences, skills and abilities.

"*I'm a fifteen-year, senior intelligence veteran of the Navy.*"

"*I am a two-year financial analyst with four years behind me as a Finance Technician in the Marines.*"

"*I have six years experience as an Air National Guard Operations Research Analyst, where I excelled in program and project management.*"

Here's a tip: Your one-minute overview could also include references to any people or places that you have in common with the networking contact:

"*ExCo is where I worked with our mutual friend, Obie Jones.*"

"*I saw that you were at BME in the last seven years. My brother was there for a few of those same years.*"

"*I got my CPE certification in 2018, working with Dottie Bryce. It's through her that I was connected to you.*"

There's always flexibility in how you present yourself.
All examples are only meant to be a guideline.
If you like them, use them! If you want to put
your own flair on it, do so!

REAL-WORLD PERSPECTIVE

Dina is a manager for a finance firm who is frequently asked to network. Here are her thoughts when an overview is muddled.

"It's disheartening. I know that people in the armed services gain great skills, but if I'm unable to discern what those are because they're unable to tell me, it's over before it starts."

On the service side is Elizabeth, who has worked with transitioning service members for the last five and a half years. Married to a Colonel in the Army, she and the family have moved eleven times in seventeen years to nine different states. Now the manager of a large U.S. Chamber Of Commerce Foundation program that connects veterans, service members, and military spouses with employment opportunities at large organizations, she works with hundreds of service members per year.

Your translation "is extremely crucial," she says. "You're bringing a whole armed-services culture with you to a meeting. You can't expect a company to understand that culture in a matter of minutes. Instead, you've got to change *your* entire mindset. You must learn to write, speak, and think 'civilian-ese.' It's not just about the resume, it's about how you network and interview, too. If they can't understand you, you're not going to make it to the next round."

BOTTOM LINE: Keep it brief, but structured. Balance your overview. Yes, you may have some translation work to do, and yes a minute is a relatively short time, but by reading the above, it should be clear how quickly, efficiently, and accurately you can describe your work history. Just practice. Rehearse. Time yourself. You will be surprised at what you can convey in just sixty seconds.

TIP: Need a kick-start to your recalling your services experiences? Obtain or review a copy of your discharge papers. (DD-214 Form; Certificate of Release; Discharge from Active Duty, among other names. Dig in!)

SAMPLES OF ONE-MINUTE OVERVIEWS

Here are some fully articulated One-Minute Overviews. Suggestion: Read them out loud and time them.

EXAMPLE 1— CAMERON

"Thank you again for taking the time to meet with me, Ryan. I thought I'd give you a quick overview of my background for some context. I was in the Army for five years, right out of high school. After two more years in the reserves, I started to really focus on career. In the Army, I was called a Nodal Network Systems Operator or Maintainer. It's the equivalent of a network administrator or IT director, and pretty hands on with installation and maintenance of network and nodal systems, including computers and telecommunications out in the field. Our discussion is part of my research to learn where my skill set fits in the Wi-Fi and 5G industries."

How did that sound? Simple, clear translation and easy to understand. Speaking that overview out loud takes around thirty seconds—plenty of time to work with!

EXAMPLE 2— EMILIO

"Nice to meet you in person, Antonia! I'm happy to explain any-thing on my resume, but I thought I'd give you a quick snapshot as a starting point. I spent eight years in the Marine Corps as a Staff Non-Commissioned Officer, which is something like a senior manager or director. I received formal Leadership training and education at NCO Academy, and oversaw the training and project accomplishment of two sergeants—or managers—and their teams, roughly two dozen people in total. This will be the first time I bring my management skills to the civilian sector, and I'd like to get your perspective on a few things."

How about that one? Around thirty-two seconds! Imagine what you can fill in with almost twice the time!

Note: If you don't have any civilian experience as of yet, no problem; you can say so, just like the above. But take care that you are clear in your translation of skills, using terms people are familiar with, so that your contacts may easily understand where you fit in the working world.

A special note on title translation: Title translation can some-times be tricky, even for civilians. That's because a Manager in a $1 billion company could possibly be a Director level in a $500 million company, holding more seniority. And vice-versa; one can go from a Director level in a smaller company, and be considered less senior when moving to a larger one. What this means is that your own title translation may sound different from company to company, or from contact to contact when you have your meet-ings. Be sure to research accordingly!

REMINDERS: For an exercise in how to put together a one-minute overview, turn to page 150 (It will walk you through the process). And—page 163 contains translation resources!

Step 3 —
Great Discussion

GOAL:	Have a short but great discussion
TIME LIMIT:	12–15 minutes
WHAT YOU WILL DO:	Talk through Five Key Questions You will draft Key Questions 1–3 yourself, using *The 20-Minute Networking Meeting* structure. Then, I will tell you exactly what to ask in Question 4 and Question 5. *(We'll get to specifics in a second. Here's some prep first.)*
NOTE:	Turn to page 157 for your Great Discussion Planner

GREAT DISCUSSION

As you can deduce, most of *The 20-Minute Networking Meeting* is spent in discussion. Still, you shouldn't spend any more than fifteen minutes in this part of the meeting. Admittedly, a robust discussion can—and typically *does*—last more than twelve to fifteen minutes, but to respect the other person's schedule, and to keep to your promise, be flexible, but stay on target. Again, the only exception is if your contact is leading the discussion, and it seems rude or counterproductive to get things back on track. In that case, just let things flow for a few extra minutes. But pay attention for signs indicating your contact is ready to wrap up the meeting. Remember: You can always meet again in the future!

WHAT YOU SHOULD KNOW

THIS IS IMPORTANT: During your meeting, never, under any circumstances, ask for information that you should already know. We alluded to this earlier in the book, but it bears repeating. This includes general info about your contact's company, the economy, political climate, news reports, or anything that a newspaper or the Internet could readily tell you.

THE REASON: Your contact reads the papers too and, like you, probably is aware of the business happenings in your region and the general business climate overall. But how unfortunate (embarrassing) would it be if you were completely clueless about such information (especially concerning your contact's organization)? You are there hoping to make a good impression!

On the other hand, with such busy schedules, your contacts might have far less time to learn what's happening with specific organizations, new products, up-and-coming sectors, or possibly (believe it or not) the trends happening right in his or her own industry.

Think about it—could this have been *you* at some point? Were you always in-the-know of what was happening in the service? Probably not. Are you familiar with the latest social networking trends, newest changes in technology or the latest happenings in the civilian market? What about thought leaders and visionaries in your chosen profession? Probably not all the time. That's the way it works. So why would it be any different for your busy networking contact?

WHAT TO DO: Improve your knowledge. Research these categories *beforehand*—and never ask about them during the meeting:

- The overall economy and business climate
- The job market
- Political changes that affect your industry or job function
- Generally available information about your industry or job function
- Readily available information about the organization and the person you're meeting with

KNOW THE PERSON YOU'RE TALKING TO

It's extremely disappointing when someone comes to meet with me and doesn't really know who I am or what I do. Most professionals feel the same, and will pass on the opportunity to help that person. As much as possible, you should know the person you're talking to.

THE REASON: It's rude if you're unfamiliar with the person you're asking assistance from. You somehow believed they could help you, yet you know nothing about them?

One of my professional friends, Barney, is about as well-connected as they come, and as a consultant he is often asked to meet for networking. He too notices when people have not done their homework before getting together.

"If someone asks to meet with me and starts by saying, 'So, what do you do?'" he says, "Our meeting suddenly becomes awfully short!"

WHAT TO DO: More research.

Here are a few things someone would learn about me from my bio on my company website:

- My job title and specialty areas
- How long I have been with my firm
- The other jobs I have had
- My educational background
- Nonprofit boards that I serve on
- Professional memberships and certifications I have

As you can see, that's a lot of fodder for great discussion, taken directly from my company bio. And that's just from the company website alone! If the individual also checked my LinkedIn page, he or she would have learned even more, including:

- The number of years I spent at each of my previous employers, along with my actual job titles
- Some of my professional interests (i.e., what LinkedIn groups I belong to)
- How networked I am (i.e., how many people I am linked with)
- People we know in common
- Professional books I've endorsed
- People I've recommended
- And a lot more!

Now, your contact might *not* have this level of information readily available, but in the age of social media, it's rare to find absolutely nothing about your contact someplace online. Take the time to get to know the person you're meeting with.

REAL-WORLD PERSPECTIVE

Quinn is a business owner and frequent networking contact who shares my belief in the importance of good planning. When professionals don't take the time to learn who she is and what she does before a networking meeting, it's a big disappointment.

"When I meet with people, I ask them whether they have visited my company's website." When the occasional networker admits that she or he hasn't, Quinn, none too shy with her feelings or thoughts, asks, "Why not?"

The message here is obvious, but if you don't like the idea of being put on the spot, be prepared. Even Quinn hopes that by asking such a potentially embarrassing question, the networker will not make the same mistake in future meetings.

KNOW THE COMPANY

It's safe to assume that when it comes to networking, a contact's company is just as important as the contact. That's to say, help from a contact in a different industry—or from a contact at a consulting company, or from someone who is unemployed—might come in a format different than that of a peer or colleague in the same industry. But if the company is a fast-growing Fortune 500, for example, it gives a lot of weight to who your contact is and what role he or she plays in the organization. So, again, knowing about the company is just as important as knowing about your contact, regardless of the organization's size.

THE REASON: It was mentioned before, but imagine how unfortunate (embarrassing) it would be to arrive at your contact's office without knowing what the company does.

WHAT TO DO: Research. Here are some examples of things you should know. (But don't limit yourself to these!):

- Recent important events
- Press releases
- Key customers
- New product introductions
- Milestones
- Pending deals
- Positive news write-ups

HOW TO DO IT: The web is a miraculous source of information. Many company websites contain press releases that will detail recent events and even mention new customers or business relationships. They, of course, will also mention new products (if that's not the first thing you see on the website).

◇◇

With so much information readily available on the web, and with so many convenient ways to access it, there's no excuse going into a networking meeting uninformed. Do your research!

◇◇

KEEP IN MIND: The more you know, the better the impression you will leave. Now, that's not to say you need to have a night of memorization before your morning meeting, but knowing key points that are important to the organization (milestones, pending deals, positive news write-ups) can only help. Just think: How flattered would *you* be if someone came to your meeting knowing something meaningful about your service background, your experience and the things you've helped your company, wing, department or district accomplish—even before you met them? Wouldn't you be more willing to help this person? If you didn't think about it yet, you can also see how this will help create an evangelist.

***

There are five questions that will provide the structure for the discussion part of your networking meeting. Before we get to them, we must discuss some questions that you should never ask. These are the questions that have become the boring standard in business and networking meetings. They're not necessarily deal-breakers, but they will define you as the same as any other networker who didn't "have the time" or put forth the effort to do some home-work. Avoid these, and you will stand out in good fashion.

Here they are. (Some of these repeat things we've already talked about, but there's no hurt in re-reminding.)

- **As mentioned, do not ask questions about things you should already know.** This includes what the contact's company does, how business has been lately, things about the economy, well-known trends in your industry, and so on. You could, however, ask for your contact's reaction to something you've read or heard on a given topic. It's always good to encourage thoughts and opinions of a contact.
- **Do not ask for work history or background overview.** Your contact is not being interviewed—don't make him or her feel that way, especially if you're the one looking for work. Find out the person's background yourself!
- **Do not ask how the two of you are connected.** You should already know this. It's your responsibility to remind your

contact about personal or professional connections.

- **Do not ask "What do you think about my resume?"** Unless they've offered to discuss it, it can put someone on the spot. It's also not relevant. Why? *You're* not being interviewed, either. Even a Human Resources or hiring professional would not appreciate this question, as resume review is rarely part of their job responsibilities. An appropriate person to ask for resume feedback would be an outplacement counselor or a job coach.
- **Do not ask personal questions without a purpose.** "Do you have children?" is not a suggested icebreaker. Respect the boundary between personal and professional questions.
- **Do not ask the contact to divulge any information about the organization that should not be shared in a relatively new relationship,** such as specific plans for upcoming layoffs, upcoming product launches, personnel changes, and the like.

REAL-WORLD PERSPECTIVE

Remember Barney, my well-connected consultant friend? Barney evaluates the level of preparation a jobseeker has put into the meeting. He anticipates that the person has "pre-thought" the meeting and therefore is "able to comment on what they have learned about me, my company, my profession." The amount of preparation affects Barney's willingness to share leads and suggest other professionals to call.

"None of my connections would ever hire someone unprepared for an interview," Barney explained. "A networking meeting, to me, is a clear indicator how someone would act in a future interview."

Even if your approach would be different, would you be willing to risk that impression?

FIVE KEY QUESTIONS: QUESTIONS 1 - 3

Your first three questions are intended to guide the very important discussion portion of your networking meeting. A short, productive meeting can be difficult for many jobseekers. But with a little thought and practice, you'll not only lead your meetings, but control its direction too.

So how do you have a meaningful discussion that is still clean and crisp while you're networking? By formulating your first three questions from the research you've done before the meeting.

You will create these key questions following the *20MNM* structure. What you ask will be completely up to you, but they must be constructed for the contact you're meeting with, according to your networking goals.

Why? To gain the unique wisdom or specific knowledge that you wish to learn from this particular contact. These are never questions that address common knowledge, or something that could be found during your prep work. Instead, they are thought-out, courteously asked inquiries specific to your contact that, perhaps, only your contact could answer.

Where's a good starting point for such carefully designed questions? Your contact's bio or LinkedIn profile, or even the contact's company website.

No such resource available on your contact? Then familiarize yourself with their profession and company so that you may ask informed questions that will ultimately inform your discussion. Read through the material carefully. The moment you wonder about something, jot it down. From here you can formulate dynamic, thought-provoking questions.

Here's such a scenario:

You're perusing your contact's LinkedIn profile and realize that he or she has certifications that you've considered getting. Formulating a question around this will not only give you something to talk about, but will provide a solid piece of information that will help you in the future.

HOW TO STRUCTURE THESE QUESTIONS

These specific contact questions come in two parts. The first part is an **observation** (or a piece of information), and the second part is the **related question** (or a request for comments from the contact).

Here is an example for the above scenario.

*"Nik, you got a Bachelor of Science in MIS (**observation**). Did that set you on a path of managing people (**related question**)?"*

Make sense? You've pointed out your observation and then you've asked a thought-provoking question related to it. Here are more examples:

*"You were a high school counselor for a few years before going into the Navy (**observation**). Knowing what you now know about the civilian business world before and after, what is a strategic step for someone leaving active duty (**related question**)?"*

*"You've worked as a financial analyst for two different companies. (**observation**). Do you suppose that a CFA certification is necessary for all kinds of financial support*

*work (**related question**)?"*

*"I'd like to ask your opinion about franchises. You started with a more traditional business background before opening your own (**observation**). Is that a recommended route, or are there other ways to learn how to run a new business (**related question**)?"*

*"Early on, you spent ten years in maintenance and repair (**observation**). Did you find that your experience set you up for the mechanical work you're doing now (**related question**)? Was there a hard lesson that you learned that could make that transition easier for me (**related question**)?"*

*"You're a Coast Guard veteran (**observation**). As a former Marine, I feel I could capitalize on my team-work experience in the civilian workforce (**observation**). Do you feel that's been the case for you (**related question**)? How has your service team experience impacted your professional relationships (**related question**)?"*

WHAT THE STRUCTURE DOES

Placing the *observation* at the beginning of your questions establishes the fact or point you're addressing. This gives the listener the heads-up as to where you're going. The *related question*, in turn, evokes the person's assistance, thereby sparking discussion. In simpler terms: You give a heads-up about *what* you're going to ask, then you ask for thoughts.

∞∞

TIP:

Asking a second related question, as in the last two examples, is perfectly acceptable. However, it's important to remember that your meeting is not a question-answer session. Sometimes it's best (even strategic) to let your contact answer your first question before you follow up with your second question—if they didn't already answer it in the process of answering the first. This way you won't put your contact on the spot or give the impression that you have a list of questions to answer. It also helps bring more depth to your discussion by delving further into your topic.

◇◇◇

◇◇◇

ANOTHER TIP:

Sometimes you can reuse your great discussion questions in multiple networking meetings. This might be valuable if, for example, you would like to get more than one perspective on a matter of great interest to you in your search. You must still think carefully about the questions you select for each networking meeting. Don't ask similar questions for lack of planning!

◇◇◇

REAL-WORLD PERSPECTIVE

Sophie is the president of a consortium of companies in the steel manufacturing industry.

"I do a fair bit of networking as part of my job leading a large trade association. My association posts some positions on our website, and I am often privy to other openings on a somewhat confidential basis.

"While I don't mind taking the meetings, I am constantly surprised by how poorly prepared some of the networkers are. People show up and are very happy about the meeting and pleasant to talk to, which seems to make the meeting go a little long. I don't have a problem with that, but I do have a problem when people arrive without a sense of who I am or what my company does. The lack of preparation renders them less able to manage the meeting effectively, and—here is my hot button—when someone requests a meeting with me and spends the time asking me about my own background, it can feel like I'm being interviewed! I wonder if these people do this in their real jobs—do they call meetings and show up unprepared and let the other person do the talking? I mean, how long would it take to do some basic planning ahead of time? Sometimes it's as though jobseekers seem to lose their ability to plan along with losing their job. It's extremely frustrating."

FIVE KEY QUESTIONS: QUESTION 4

Your fourth question will help you with a major objective for the meeting: expanding your network. Essentially, you'll be asking your contact to recommend the names of some individuals whom you can reach out to. This question will be similar each time you ask it, but slightly tailored on a case-by-case basis. The gist is to ask for further networking contacts.

This is where networking breaks down for jobseekers at all experience levels, even executives. It's where I've seen a lot of people freak out. The general consensus is: *"It was hard enough asking for the meeting itself! If I ask for names of other people, I'm gonna seem pushy or desperate."*

That's not true. Rest assured, that's how *successful* business works—give-and-take. Also, this feeling (and the excuses that come with it) isn't unusual, so there's nothing to worry about here. In fact, I've heard these same protests for as long as I can remember (along with, *"No one wants to give names of other people,"* and, *"This part is just too uncomfortable!"*). But not a day of business goes by when people aren't doing this very thing on every level in every industry out there. Whether civilians or veterans. Looking at it from that standpoint, there's no reason to avoid asking the question.

Having said that, I want to acknowledge that getting started isn't all that easy. So, here are a couple of tips to deal with the fear.

- Remind yourself that the people you meet with have also had to find a job at one time too. Some more than once. They know the value of networking. They get it.
- Remind yourself that these people said *yes* to a meeting with you in the first place. They likely know that you will be asking for names of contacts.
- Because they know the drill, they may even have come prepared with some names in mind.

REAL-WORLD PERSPECTIVE

Jerlyn is a business owner who often meets with professionals in her industry. She told me that she expects a networking meeting to include a request for other contacts.

"I come prepared with some ideas," she told me. "But the 'ask' is important, too. I won't give the names without the question."

WHAT HAPPENS IF THEY SAY NO?

Well, then they say no (which is the worst that can happen). A gracious thank you will suffice, and then you simply move on to your fifth and final question.

Let's get to some examples. If the general question that you want to ask is "Who else do you know that might be a good contact for me in my job search?" you could probably go ahead and just say as much. But put a little more consideration behind it, and you might get a much better response.

Here are some ways to ask:

"Do you know of someone else with a web developer background who might answer the same questions I asked you?"

"Do you know of another security systems tech at a different company that might be good to call?"

"You used to work for CBA. Do you have any current or former telecommunications colleagues from there whom I could touch base with?"

Notice the phrasing in those questions. They're direct, yet considerate. They're not blunt, but they're totally clear. Word choice is needed. Sincerity and appreciation are crucial. But it doesn't have to be anything difficult. Just give thought to your words, and rest assured that you're not the only person who has asked them before. But again, it's your gracious attitude and genuine appreciation that will make the difference.

Years ago, I got a cold call from a sales representative in the clothing business. She asked for a few minutes of my time to come in and show me her line of custom clothing. I wasn't sure if I was the custom-clothing type, but I said yes to the meeting. At the end of the meeting, I decided that I definitely was not the custom-clothing type of person and elected not to make a purchase. The meeting had been very pleasant and the sales representative had been gracious. Undaunted, she proceeded to what we are calling Question 4, but instead of directly asking, "Who else do you know that might be interested in buying from my line of custom clothing?" she asked slightly modified ones instead. Like, "Who do you know that is interested in fashion?" "Who do you know that you would describe as 'trendy'?" "Do you have any friends who drive fancy sports cars?" Had she asked me for a straight referral, I'm not sure I would have been able to deliver one. But with questions phrased in different ways, I was able to think of several possible names. Your careful phrasing can have the same outcome.

◇◇◇

Positive networking gets additional contacts.
After a professionally managed meeting, sealed with gratitude and the proper give-and-take, your contacts will be much more likely to refer you to their own contacts.

◇◇◇

FIVE KEY QUESTIONS: QUESTION 5

Now, I know we've focused a lot on how to get what you need out of a networking meeting, but we can't lose sight of what networking really is—give-and-take. And while an entire book could be written about the give-and-take philosophy, this idea is worth repeating: Networking isn't all about you (or me). It's about *both* parties.

So, the last question you must ask in a networking meeting is:

"How can I help *you*?"

Yes, I admit that this question, given the topic of this book, might seem counterintuitive. But it's directly responsible for expanding your network and making evangelists of your contacts. In fact, it's possibly the most vital component of *The 20-Minute*

Networking Meeting.

Big claims, right? Let me tell you why.

By nature, networking is something that must benefit both parties. If you think about it in armed-services terms, it's a "I've got your back, you've got mine," *sensibility.* Trust. Mutual respect. Earned reciprocity.

Also, asking to network, receiving the gift of time, and asking for new contacts without offering something in return (even with a gracious thank-you) is just bad form. Worse, such a crime of *take, take, take* is rarely forgotten. But if you find a way to give back, you not only will be bestowed "good karma," you will demonstrate a clear indication of your consideration and appreciation for the time that was given to you in the first place.

What this also means is that, over time, you will always to have the opportunity to serve others the way they have served you—with information and introductions to others that help them achieve their endeavors, whatever those maybe.

Besides standing out from the pack, here's a few other things that consideration and appreciation could get you:

→ *Reciprocated* respect and consideration (Who doesn't want to help someone who helps *them?*)

WHICH COULD LEAD TO:

→ An *additional* networking meeting with that contact

→ A meeting in a different part of the same organization

WHICH COULD LEAD TO:

→ An additional name that your contact was reluctant to give up at first (Sometimes networking contacts question whether they want to give away names, but gratitude and appreciation tip the scale.)

WHICH COULD LEAD TO:

→ A wider network (Translation: more word of mouth about *you* in the marketplace.) Which could lead to:

→ An evangelist

→ A consulting/part-time gig

→ A great reputation as a thoughtful businessperson

→ And the best of all: a job opportunity!

SO HOW DO YOU PHRASE THE QUESTION?

By saying it directly. "How can I help *you*?"

Of course it could be phrased a few other ways too, but asking in an off-handed manner doesn't come across as sincere, nor does it suggest actual consideration. And no one is going to be sincere with you if you're not sincere with them. Just be direct and mean it. It will pay off.

WHAT IF THEY'RE TAKEN BY SURPRISE?

This is sure to happen. As I mentioned, it's rare for people to offer help in return for help, right? Be prepared by having done your research. Here are some scenarios:

"Thanks so much for the time and information you've given me, Esme. Now, how can I help you?"

Esme gives you a look of shock.

"Gosh, Darin, I guess I can't think of anything at the moment."

But, you know how important it is to give, and if you have done your research, you'll know what to do.

What would that be, you ask? Read on for some possibilities:

"Well, you mentioned border security. My program manager, Georgina, wrote a report on the Coast Guard and border security. I would be happy to connect you two."

"I saw the hunting photos on your wall. I grew up fowl hunting. I can send you a list of where to stay for guided trips."

"My friend (uncle/father/aunt) is a professional plumber. How about if I send over some contact information and material about sink installations?"

"Hiking has always been my favorite pastime. How about if I send you a handful of web links that point out the walk-in trailheads?"

And if there seems to be nothing you could help with right at that moment, have a backup:

"Well, Avril, thank you again for your time and thoughts. If you think of anything I can help with in the future, please let me know. Still, as a token of appreciation for your time, I brought a copy of Easter Island. Maybe you'll find it interesting given your work in ancient history."

Note: You could only pull something like that off if you have done your research. If you don't know what's going on in your contact's organization, such a move is a lot less effective, or maybe ineffective. *Do your research!*

Summary

No matter whom you meet with and no matter what you talk about, just be sure to end your meeting with Question 5, "How can I help *you?*"

Why end with it? Because it will leave your contact with a solid final impression of you, should your meeting get interrupted or end early. Let that impression be one of consideration and appreciation—that you are gracious and grateful. Everyone is proud to know of such a thoughtful, considerate person. Better yet, people want to help one when they can.

Remember: the power of this question can make people remember you fondly, which in turn can make them think of you first, professionally. Always ask "How can I help *you?*"

REAL-WORLD PERSPECTIVE

Naomi is a public and corporate affairs leader for a Fortune 500 company. She had the following reaction when a job-seeking networker asked, "What can I do to help you?"

"I about fell out of my chair," she said. "No one had ever asked me that."

But the reciprocity, surprise, and the power of that question didn't stop there. Allowing herself to accept the offer, the networking favor was returned.

"Knowing I might be leaving in a few months due to layoffs, I asked the person if they could connect me with someone at another organization. They did."

According to Naomi many things changed after that day, including the fact that the original networker who requested to meet with Naomi, "has been a valuable part of my network ever since."

And what about now? Is anything different?

"It was such a poignant moment for me when that question was asked," that Naomi has begun the practice herself. The response she gets?

"The response is often a 'stunned silence.' And when I suggest a couple ways (to help)—sending an article, helping them connect with someone in my network—the person opens up," giving more information, and at times, additional names.

How's that for the power of offering to help in return? And that's coming from an executive whose expertise is media, government, and community communications!

THE IMPORTANCE OF GIVING

Then there's the flip side. While thinking about this book, and wanting to put its concept and message into practice, I agreed to meet with a C-level (chief executive; chief financial; chief operations, etc.) executive who requested a networking meeting with me. The person was referred by someone I respect, so I figured this was as solid a setup as I could ask for.

We made an appointment, and she arrived at the appropriate date and time. So far, so good. Then she jumped in by telling me about the types of jobs that she wanted. (Remember: networking contacts are not a grocery store, and they're not your immediate pathway to your next job. Hiring managers and recruiters operate in accordance with hiring necessities, not a candidate's hiring desires.) I looked through her resume and offered some recommendations and referrals, and very quickly, twenty minutes had elapsed.

Then, I turned the table. I told her that, if we could, I was hoping the second part of the meeting could include helping me. I told her I was interested in some leadership programs she had attended and some executive groups she belonged to. I wanted to spend a few minutes picking her brain about those topics for my benefit.

Well, despite the fact that this was a *networking* meeting

(which means it goes both ways—give-and-take, remember), the meeting stopped cold. There was a look of almost shock on her face. She hadn't even considered the idea of mutuality or helping the other person. I kept my own questions brief, and the discussion continued cordially. But I learned something that day. Many folks who network have still not picked up on the concept of giving back. My suggestion: Be different. Bring an attitude of helpfulness.

Turn to page 153 for examples of some actual items you might give as a token of your gratitude.

Step 4 —
Great Ending

GOAL:	Make a great final impression
TIME LIMIT:	2 minutes
WHAT YOU WILL DO:	Review any action, express more gratitude, *wrap it up*!

GREAT ENDING

Every great beginning has a great ending. Now that you have reviewed your background with your contact, managed the robust discussion between the two of you, and found a way to be helpful in return, you're ready to conclude the meeting. What's most important in this case is doing so in a clear manner.

REMINDER: Your 20-minute networking meeting is probably shorter than what your contact was prepared for, which is to say that your contact, while appreciating your meeting management skills, still might be expecting a longer session. Be clear when the meeting is done.

Here are some examples:

"That's all I have to ask. Thanks again, Tyrion, for your time. I'm grateful for your thoughts."

"Well, I will let you get back to your workday, Rosannah. Thanks so much for meeting with me."

"My time is up, Cait. You've been really gracious. Thank you."

Just like any of the past examples, these wrap-ups can be modified to fit your style, so long as you hit the most critical point: showing your gratitude and sincere appreciation.

HOW TO DO IT

There are two quick steps to the great ending: recapping what you and your contact will do next, and saying *thank you* a final time.

FIRST: REVIEW ACTIONS

After you indicate that you are ending the meeting, you'll want to review any actions or next steps from the session. It'll sound something like these:

"Thank you for offering to introduce me to Major Ainsley, I look forward to hearing about his civilian transition. Once I'm back at my computer, I'll send you the calendar for the veteran soccer league."

"Okay, I'll introduce you to my cousin Marisa by email first thing in the morning. She's been in financial services for awhile, so I know she can answer your budget questions. And I look forward to meeting your recruiter contact, Arn. Thanks again for setting that up."

"Okay, to recap: I'll send an email with Matthew's information and will forward the resume of the Army engineer

that I said might be good for your construction business. And, I really am grateful that you will keep your eyes and ears open for any contract jobs you might hear about. Thank you."

Notice that they all express gratitude and address "next steps." Also note that they are clear indicators that the end of the meeting has come.

SECOND: EXPRESS MORE GRATITUDE

I know gratitude has been mentioned a lot over the course of this book, but I often find that it is critically undervalued in every day business. Please don't make this mistake. People appreciate being appreciated. And in the end, it will matter to you and your job search.

Here are some things that you'll probably be thankful for:

- Their expertise
- Their time
- Their wisdom
- Their suggestions
- Their introductions
- Their referrals
- Their willingness to help you at all

How about a few examples in expressing more gratitude?

"Deven, I see we went over by ten minutes, but thank you for the extra time. I had no idea that your company was opening a facility near where I was stationed. I will be in touch with an updated resume in two weeks."

"Wow, Noelene, coming out of the service, this information is invaluable. Thank you for everything you've shared about the veteran recruitment process here, and in general. I learned a ton."

"I value your thoughts, Buster, thank you for your time. These are challenging things to think about, but I know it's going to make me a better candidate during my job search. Thank you again."

REAL-WORLD PERSPECTIVE

Marine veteran Corbin began utilizing *The 20-Minute Networking Meeting* a few months after leaving active service. He commented on what gratitude and humility did for his networking.

"I saw a change in people from my earlier meetings," he explained. "I could immediately see that being appreciative for someone's time almost always had a positive outcome for me. I got more meetings, and built stronger relationships."

Though Corbin is employed now, he said that he has taken his attitude of gratitude into the workplace with him. It continues to pay off, he says.

"I'm still in touch with people I networked with before I got a job. Some may even become clients in time. Some have become friends. It's because of my long-standing relationship with them. I know it started with gratitude for our meetings."

WRAP-UP

While we've made clear that you have a lot to cover in a good wrap-up, that doesn't mean it should turn into a long goodbye. Remember, leave them wanting more. A brief but positive goodbye is all you need. Then you're set!

Step 5 —
Great Follow-Up

GOAL:	Follow up after the meeting
TIME LIMIT:	Varies
WHAT YOU WILL DO:	Take prompt action to follow up after the meeting
NOTE:	Turn to page 161 for your Great Follow-Up Tracker

GREAT FOLLOW-UP

We're nearly at the end of our networking journey together. Even so, these final pages should not be overlooked. Keeping in touch after your meetings is crucial to keeping your network alive over time. As Army Veteran, and Veteran Career Advisor Alan Hill says "This is your network. You're responsible for them - just like your troops. They are yours now. Show you care about them."

Why such a big deal to follow up?

It's yet another way to show appreciation for your contact's gift of time. Equally important, and already mentioned—it's how to keep your network alive over time. Here's a look at what's involved.

WHAT TO DO: You should keep track of everything. *Everything.*

THE REASON: Keeping track of everything (by keeping excellent notes) will allow you to back-reference your conversations, your communications, and any pertinent points of information that you should mention in your follow-up. Specific messages are far more appreciated and effective than a simple thank-you and signature. Why? Because it leaves an impression of sincerity that you took your original networking meeting(s) to heart. Your notes will also help make your follow-up faster and more efficient. With everything already jotted down, you won't have to search your mind for thoughtful things to mention, wouldn't you say?

◇◇◇

Keep track of *everything*. A solid set of notes will help you back-reference any pertinent points of information that you should mention in your follow-up. It builds trust and a sense of reliability. Plus, it's faster and more efficient.

◇◇◇

Here are some examples of what to keep track of. Be sure to write these things down the moment they happen!

- **Your phone calls.** If you speak with a contact by phone, write down the person's name and what you talked about (and that it was by phone). Keep track of things that strike you as important, new, or informative to your job search.
- **Your meeting dates.** Always be able to reference when you met, with whom you met, and what you talked about.

- **All correspondence.** Include time of original contact and responses.
- **Your follow-up messages.** (Yes, even your follow-up messages.) You should be able to look back at your notes and know each time that you have followed up. Keeping track of your messages will also help you maintain a timeline of correspondence. This will help you gauge when it's appropriate to reach out again in the future.
- **All other pertinent information** that you've learned along the way. Sometimes someone will say something that really sticks out to you. There's no better way to make an evangelist out of a contact than having such small, but pertinent points, quotes, or pieces of information at your fingertips.

Here are some common pitfalls to avoid:

"I will be employed soon. There won't be much need for follow-up because I will be in a job before you know it."

WHY TO AVOID THIS MENTALITY: Though this could be the case, what if it doesn't happen as quickly as you expect? Besides, for any number of reasons (such as career growth, career transition, industry change, personal circumstances), you may very well want this written information months, even years down the line.

"I've got a good memory. I don't need to track my follow-up communications, because I'll just remember it all."

WHY TO AVOID THIS MENTALITY: Networking can involve scores or even hundreds of people. Remembering dates, locations, topics, mutual connections, and personal or professional interests is going to become a major issue. Don't forget, when you meet a contact, all that person has to remember is *you* (which will be easy if you have a successful first meeting). However, *you* will have to remember all of your contacts, and all the pieces of information they give to you. How embarrassing would it be if you can't remember that person's suggestions and advice? Worse, if you can't remember the *person*?

> *"I'm more of a spontaneous worker. I'll just follow up on the fly."*

WHY TO AVOID THIS MENTALITY: Forgetting information or to follow up with a contact (who freely gave their time to help you) is inconsiderate. Worse, it can damage trust and others' sense of your reliability. Instead, reinforce the positive impression that you create in your meetings by letting your contacts see that you're taking notes. It will build trust, and that, along with reliability, is what makes evangelists.

Special note: When taking notes, consider using a good old-fashioned notepad. Avoid the misperception that you may be focused on something else if using a device.

REAL-WORLD PERSPECTIVE

A company owner I know frequently takes time to meet with job-seekers. He appreciates getting a follow-up message right away.

"It only takes a few minutes," he told me. "I don't know why you wouldn't do it. I've had to search for a job, too. And I've even hired people I've met through networking. If you want to stay in someone's mind, follow up. If you don't, you won't."

THE KINDS OF FOLLOW-UP

Believe it or not, there are two kinds of follow-up. First, we'll deal with the immediate follow-up, and then we'll focus some attention on ongoing follow-up.

IMMEDIATE FOLLOW-UP

- First person to follow up with:
    the networking contact you just met with
- Second person to follow up with:
    the networking contact who referred you

HOW TO FOLLOW UP: By sending a thank-you. A hand-written note is always preferred (it's uncommon in the digital age, and leaves a great impression), but an email will work too, so long as you do either one right away.

Here is an example of a follow-up note to a networking contact:

Dear Glenna,

It was great to meet you this morning. I hadn't considered that there could be more of a "family" feel to working in a smaller business. As you know, working in a team environment where my ideas are valued, is important to me. Thank you.

And last, congratulations on seeing your son off to college! As I mentioned, I can serve as a resource when he moves to Denver. I was stationed at Buckley Air Force Base in Aurora, and I know the city and region well.

Kind regards,

Leesa Hadley

And another:

Dear Lovel,

Thank you for meeting with me this past Tuesday. I've already seen a change in email responses, and I'm sure it's because of my expressions of gratitude. Even with people I already know! Thank you for pointing out the importance of this!

Also, there is a church event meant for civilians and veterans next Saturday. Live polka, barbecue for the family. :) I'll send you the invite.

Thanks again,

Winston Noble

YOUR REFERRING CONTACT

Thanking your contacts is always a must-do, but sending gratitude to the contact who referred you to your new contact is also very important. Considering this is how a network is expanded, and ultimately how work is obtained, it's an essential part of the chain. Never forget to loop back to your referring contact with a thank-you for the introduction to your new contact!

Here is an example of a thank-you message addressed to your referring contact:

Dear Jade,

Thank you so much for introducing me to Lynn Davey. We met this afternoon, and wow—he gave me three different ideas that I can run with.

I'll be in touch with an update in the weeks or months to come, but in the meantime, please let me know if there is anything I can do for you in return for your help.

Art Parker

Here's another example:

Dear Wenda,

Thank you for the LinkedIn introduction to Stella Brinley. We met yesterday for a quick coffee. A good friend of hers is a Project Designer in commercial construction, which is exactly what I'm looking to do after the Army Corp of Engineers. She has already introduced us by email. Thank you again for introducing us—I don't see how I could have made this connection without you. I'll send an update soon.

By the way—you mentioned possible building construction at the office. As you now know, I have eight years of USACE experience behind me, and I'm happy to help with any advice you may need.

Kind regards,

Sammie Bryson

◇◇

Don't let more than twenty-four hours pass
before sending a thank-you follow-up.
Much longer makes it seem like an afterthought!

◇◇

ONGOING FOLLOW-UP

So, what is ongoing follow-up if not continued contact? Well, it's actually networking maintenance. Many times, networkers send their thanks and gratitude and think that's that. This is acceptable, but it doesn't help expand or strengthen their network. And if you've noted anything by now, it's that a healthy, vibrant network is essential to job-search and business success.

WHAT TO DO: If you have meaningful reasons to check back or update a contact or contacts, then do so!

But how does one continue to follow up, you ask? And how often is appropriate? These are common questions, and the answers are pretty straightforward. Read on.

WHEN TO BE IN TOUCH

- **If you find an article or website** that you genuinely think the person would value. Don't ever forward something meaningless just to send a follow-up message. It can backfire. But thoughtful information, sent with good wishes and a brief update, is welcome.
- **If your contact information has changed.** If you have moved or have a new phone number or email address, you should reconnect with your network to inform them of the change. Attach an updated resume to an email message if you are still in job-search, and it's appropriate to do so.
- **If your employment status has changed,** or if you have completed a degree or earned a significant certification. Again, you should attach an updated resume if you are still in job-search, and if appropriate.
- **If you *don't* have an update that includes time-sensitive or significant information**, stay in touch about once a quarter, at most. Every few weeks is too often!

Examples:

Martha,

Thanks again for meeting with me a few months back,

and for being a part of my network. I wanted to share that I (finally!) got my Class B driver's license. This qualifies me to drive anything over 26,001 pounds, meaning 16-passenger vehicles and similar. Attached is my updated resume reflecting the change. If you hear of anyone looking to hire, or if I can help you in any way, please let me know.

Have a great weekend!

Willy

Additional reasons for ongoing follow-up:

- **If you are thinking about the person and want to say hello.** Sometimes a nicely worded message to say hi is okay, but it should not be done too often; it can be received more as social or even bothersome and not professional. Use judgment.

- **If your networking introduces you to someone** who is closely connected with your contact. People enjoy it when a mutual connection is shared. When the world becomes smaller, trust is built. A word of advice, though: you should be sure about the relationship. I've had plenty of people call me and proudly tell me that they were referred to me by a "friend" of mine. Unfortunately, I frequently don't know the supposed "friend" who has connected us.

- **If you want to further discuss something mentioned in the meeting.** Perhaps your meeting revealed that you and your contact are both watching a certain start-up company or the publication of a new book by an author in your field.

How about:

Tottie,

Thanks again for meeting with me this summer. I hope you had the super humid season you were looking for! (How do you handle it?)

In case you didn't catch this article about the White River, I've attached a copy. It reminded me of our kayaking conversation, and it looks like the "Amazon-y" water trail you're looking for!

Your advice was much appreciated and has continued to help my job search. Thank you again. Please let me know if I can be of assistance to you!

Shanon Briar

One more:

- **If you have news to share** about someone you both know (a promotion, new company, an award, etc.)

Joella,

It was great getting coffee with you last month. In case you didn't already see it in the local paper, Isador, who referred me to you as a networking contact, was honored with a Small Business Award. I'm attaching a flyer about the party in case you hadn't received one. Maybe I will see you there!

Kind regards,

Dashielle Headley

><><><><><><><><><><><><><><><><><><><><><><><><><><><><><><><><><><><>

Unless you have an update including time-sensitive or significant information, consider staying in touch about once a quarter, at most. Every few weeks is too often!

><><><><><><><><><><><><><><><><><><><><><><><><><><><><><><><><><><><>

THE KIND OF FOLLOW-UP YOU *DON'T* DO

- **Mass emails** where the email addresses of all parties are visible. (This one is horrible. It is impersonal. It also shows just how many people you're not taking seriously.) Instead, take the time to personalize each message. After all, people have networked with you one-on-one, so stay in touch in the same way.
- **Too-frequent updates** with only minuscule changes in your situation to report.
- **Stories, quotes, or platitudes** about general topics. Some job-searchers who have run out of meaningful professional updates turn to sending generic bits about leadership or business strategy, hoping that they will be noticed and remembered. After a fashion, these types of messages, if not automatically deleted, are remembered for the wrong reasons.

Most of us value meaningful updates from people we know. Recruiters and hiring professionals are no different. We share pertinent information about people among ourselves and put the most current information into our database. On the other hand, we joke about the silly, meaningless updates we get from other folks, too. How would *you* react to a weekly email from a job-seeker containing jokes, song lyrics, philosophical quotes, ditties, and the like?

EXAMPLES OF GOOD AND BAD FOLLOW-UP

First, a good follow-up message:

Hi Everett,

Thanks again for meeting with me last month. I hope you didn't have to swim to safety after of our last rain storm.

So wow- I guess it's really a small world after all. I met your former co-worker, Laurencia Chavez, at an event for veterans. I was there with a friend who has done work with a transition group over the years. They're creating a job-search program for older and newer vets, which I'm part of. Laurencia says hey!

Just wanted to say hi. Please be in touch, or reach out with anything I can help you with.

Best regards,

Kole Lorey

Here's an example of a bad follow-up message:

Hey everyone,

I still haven't found a job yet. Keep me in mind if you hear of openings for bartender, restaurant manager, retail clerk, sales associate, call center associate or anything that pays decently. No painting or physical labor. Or forward my resume to others who can help.

Thanks for doing this for me!

Yondo Bondo

Another bad follow-up message:

To: *Mailing List*
Subject: *Gabby's Gallant Words of the Wise, Volume XII*

I know it's been a month since I've written, but here's your thoughts for November.

"If you can think it, you can do it."—Anonymous

"I am thankful for all of those who said NO to me. It's because of them I'm doing it myself." –Albert Einstein

I'm thinking a lot about myself these days, and I hope you are too!

Sincerely,

Gabby Chatsworth

And of course, what will happen if you don't follow up at all: This might sound harsh, but you'll be forgotten. If you don't stay in touch in some way, people will assume you have landed in a new job and will not continue to think of you. But again, what you don't want to do is follow up so frequently that you become a bother. It's about balance. People who have taken the time to meet with you are people who want to help you. Honor both their time and their effort with occasional, meaningful updates.

REAL-WORLD PERSPECTIVE

Jim is a business unit president at a large manufacturing corporation. When asked why he stopped accepting networking requests, this is what he had to say.

"I got sick of feeling used. I work for a company that has been voted one of our state's best places to work for five years in a row. It is totally understandable why people would want to network their way into our company.

"But here's what has bothered me. I would take the time to meet with people, then I would never hear another word. Nothing. No thank-you, no follow-up, no nothing. The worst part is seeing a notice on LinkedIn or a trade publication that the person landed in a new job months ago, and me not knowing anything about it. I'd like to feel that my small contribution somehow helped them land in a job. Maybe that's just conceit. But how long does it take to send a quick email thanking people? How long does it take to prepare and send an announcement? How long to call with a message? Certainly, less time than I took for a meeting to help you when you needed it!

"Sorry to be so rigid about it. But that is my experience. I have heard the same from others at my company. So I quit accepting these meetings altogether. I refer callers to our HR department instead."

Pulling It All Together

At this point, you should be able to see ways to put the *20MNM* into practice for your own job search. Stick with it and have faith. The *20MNM* approach has produced amazing results for veterans like you. Better meetings, better impressions, more evangelists, more opportunities, better and sooner employment.

As we cruise the home stretch, let's look at someone who experienced just this.

Mike left the military a Captain in the Marines. Early on, when he was an artillery officer in Okinawa, Japan, Mike was a forward observer, and the Battery Platoon commander responsible for the maintenance of howitzers. Tracking down parts was a challenge, he explained. Computer printouts were already new, but handheld devices soon replaced larger computers, changing the norm altogether. This gave Mike his first introduction to information systems.

After the Marines, a completed MBA in Management Information Systems and a number of years in the workforce, Mike found himself faced with a sudden, necessary job transition. Twice.

Here's Mike on how it all happened.

"I was rolling off a project where I was traveling to Detroit every week for over a year," he explained. "And I wanted to stay local. The company didn't have anything local, so they assigned me to a big national agency for my job transition out of the company. The agency helped on resume, job applications and admin stuff. We had meetings once a week. But my networking seemed limited to the people in my group. I had a couple of phone interviews with big companies, even talked with hiring managers. Then crickets. After three months, I wondered 'why is this so hard?'"

What changed?
"Two things. A Veterans group and networking. It started with a city WorkForce Center Veterans Group. What a difference. Everyone there was looking to help Veterans get a job."

And the networking?
"Well, the first Veterans group is how I met people at the Eagle Group. That's where I was encourage to read and use *The 20-Minute Networking Meeting*, which I did. Then through the people at Eagle Group, I was introduced to a new network of other veterans and non-veterans that ultimately led to my re-employment. Not just once, but twice."

How did these new meetings change your perception on networking?
"They let me see what networking should be, and that I needed to expand to everyone I knew, not just military. So then I talked with college friends, former bosses, and got contacts from them for more networking meetings and informational interviews."

What impact did that have on your search?
"I started to see real job leads immediately. And my job offer came fast – after six months of networking, I had 2 companies I really felt good about. That was starting from nowhere, nine months prior."

You said networking led to employment not once, but twice. What happened?

"Sixteen months after I joined the company, they laid off my entire group. I thought I was going to retire from there. It was a good job and good group. So I had to go out there and network for a job again. But this time I was prepared."

How?

"I had maintained my network. I had stayed active with weekly Eagle Group meetings, helping other people with job search. I called on them, and those I had networked with prior to the first job. This included a former boss, who introduced me to her boss, which resulted in a networking meeting. That was within weeks of losing my job. He sent me an application link weeks later. As there were a few more weeks of silence while things got ironed out on their side, I kept networking and job searching just in case. But I was offered the job shortly after that."

I asked Mike what he does differently now than in the past.

"I am more outgoing introducing myself – giving and getting contact information, and tracking it all. I ask everyone I meet in professional scenarios if I may be a contact of theirs, and then make a note where I know them from. And I pay it forward now that I know the value of networking for myself, too. People can use me for ideas; interview practice; whatever they need. And though I don't have jobs to offer, I have contacts at a lot of different places."

This must mean you have expanded your network.

"Yes, almost at 600 contacts now! Compared to almost nothing when I worked with that transition agency two years ago."

What else is different?

"Quite a few things. My meetings end right on, or near time. I come away with more names for other networking meetings. I research ahead of time, to know something about contacts I meet with, and I follow up with an email right away to thank people."

Have these things had positive outcomes?
"I'm still getting contacted by my network to see if I am interested in their job! But I am happy where I am – I pass these leads on to others who are still looking – everything helps!"

One Final Example

A Sample 20-Minute Networking Meeting

Let's take one last look at the principles of *The 20-Minute Networking Meeting* in action. The following pages contain a full example of what a networking meeting looks like. Of course, your meetings won't go exactly as this one does, but you'll get the gist of how things might work and, more importantly, why they work that way.

We'll follow the example with imagined Q&A sheets with our imaginary characters and give example takeaways that point out the lessons. Enjoy!

SAMPLE 20-MINUTE NETWORKING MEETING

The following scenario shows the networking interaction between Ray Burke, a recently laid off veteran, and Ollie Trent, another veteran whom Ray runs into at a career services event.

Ray Burke & Ollie Trent

Ray pushed back his chair and stood. The main event was closing down. Time to meet people. The quarterly veterans event always had great speakers and he was glad he attended, but like the past two events, his nerves were acting up and pride was getting in the way. While he really needed a job, he just wasn't feeling social. Not tonight anyway. He gathered his things and headed for the door.

As Ray left the conference room, someone called his name. Behind him was Ollie Trent. Ollie was a funny guy, a veteran, and a big supporter of veteran events. He was also one of his aunt's former co-workers. He had been to many of their family get-togethers over the years, as he used to live in the neighborhood, but it had been a while since they saw each other.

"Sergeant Burke!" Ollie said with a wry smile. They shook hands. "How's the job search going?"

Ray still wasn't comfortable talking about this.

"Pretty good," he replied. But it wasn't, and not having work was eating at him. Ray had lost his most recent job at the beginning of the summer, just eighteen months after leaving the Army. Now he was back to square one. Even buddies who had gotten jobs before him still had employment. Taking the summer off before jumping back in the job market, Ray was now regretting taking the break.

"Anything promising?" Ollie asked as they walked through the building.

It was as good a time as any. It had never been easy for Ray to ask for help, but fortune wasn't going to drop in his lap. Besides, meeting people was why he was here in the first place, and he knew Ollie.

"Not yet," Ray replied. "But I'm trying to network. Like coming here." Now came the hard part. "And I'd actually really value your opinions if you have some time. Just twenty minutes."

Ray stopped at the front door. In the window reflection, he thought he saw apprehension in Ollie's expression, but it wasn't there when he turned.

"Well, we can talk longer than that, Sergeant."

"You with work, me finding work, we're all busy. Just twenty minutes."

Ollie smiled. This was new. Ray used to be pretty shy. But Ollie always saw the promise in him—everybody did—especially after the military. It was a good change.

"Of course! Let's set up a time," Ollie said. He reached for the door handle. Then: "I don't know if you thought about it, but I went through a job hunt went I got out of the service, too." He chuckled. "In fact, a few of them since. Even last year. Rough…"

Ray felt his eyebrows rise. Being so caught up in his own circumstances, he had never even considered that Ollie had gone through something like this. Last year? That would explain why he hadn't seen him in some time.

This thought gave Ray a slight sense of relief, even hope. If a vet and experienced professional like Ollie had gone through a tough job-hunt, even a few—then maybe he would be alright after all. Ollie would have a lot to offer when they met up again.

"Thank you, I really appreciate it. I'll send you an email to set things up." They shook hands.

If I'd known networking was as simple as this, Ray thought as he left the building, I'd have started weeks ago. Better late than never.

Two weeks later, Ray arrived at Ollie's building with plenty to talk about. It seemed inconceivable to show up asking for leads with no ideas of his own, so he had done his research.

Don't make Ollie run the meeting, Ray reminded himself. You're the one looking for a job.

"Come on in!" Ollie said, greeting him in the lobby. They shook hands. Ollie gestured toward a nearby break room, and Ray followed. He couldn't recall Ollie being this enthusiastic or happy, even when he worked with his aunt. Something had gone right since last year.

Ray put his belongings on the table and took a seat. He respected Ollie's busy schedule, and did not want to waste his time. He began right away.

"Thanks again for meeting with me, Ollie. I appreciate it. And as I said, I only need 20 minutes."

"No problem. It's great to see you. Besides, I want to hear how things have been going. And your aunt, by the way, how is she?"

Ollie explained that it was Delores, Clint's aunt, who was coincidentally responsible for the work he was doing now. She had connected him to a set of friends that had led to the job.

This gave Ray a renewed sense of positivity. It was encouraging to know that it happened by meeting other people that Ollie didn't know. He was learning already.

Telling himself to keep to his promise of twenty minutes, Ray got back to his agenda. *Use time wisely*, he reminded himself.

With a smile—and feeling much more comfortable—he went on.

"I was reading your LinkedIn profile and noticed that you manage the youth basketball league with my aunt's best friend, Andre Harlow. He's the one that encouraged me to talk to you in the first place, a long time ago."

"Andre!" Ollie laughed. "That guy's crazy. He and I played basketball in high school. Imagine my surprise when I saw him at your aunt's first barbecue!"

Ray laughed, feeling good that they had someone in common

besides his aunt.

Taking advantage of the momentum, he kept things rolling. Ray knew he couldn't just jump into a discussion, so he gave Ollie a lead-up.

"Okay, what I'd like to do, Ollie, is just share some of my background and situation. Then if it's okay, I have a couple of follow-up questions to get your perspective on. That's it."

Ollie nodded. Ray took a relaxing breath and continued.

"As you know, I left the army after eight years. I earned two software engineering certificates during that time. Computers are great, but I think I'm interested in using my software education someplace where I feel I'm making a difference. Like for schools, or the medical field. But I'm open to anything that helps others and helps me grow."

Ollie nodded thoughtfully, reflecting on what Ray said. Ray added, "And I just want to be clear, Ollie: I'm not asking you to find me a job. I'm just trying to familiarize myself with the territory." This is where his research came into play. "For instance, could you talk to me more about company product lines? I've done some reading, and I know you make audio components for other businesses. From an engineering perspective, do you see one sector growing faster than another? Are there product changes or trends that might change the types of companies that I should be connecting with?"

Ray could see it: Ollie's expression changed. Something clicked, and ideas were forming in his mind.

Ollie sat forward and told Ray what he knew. He mentioned that a couple of their company partners seemed to be taking a new direction, while others were expanding their current efforts. That was currently happening, he said.

For Ray, this was a major eye-opener. Such changes meant all companies could be hiring. He wrote down the information carefully, not missing a thing.

The conversation quickly transitioned to his qualifications. Then after a brief discussion about an industry certification course, Ray built the courage to ask Ollie about his own job search experience. After all, what better person to ask about the journey than someone who had already traveled the road?

"Last time we saw each other, Ollie, you mentioned being in my position at this time last year. To be honest, I've been having a tough time, and I'd appreciate hearing any lessons that you wish you'd known then. If you'd be willing to share."

Ollie nodded again, and grinned in spite of himself. Ray was asking questions that he *himself* should have asked during his job search. Had he done so, he knew he would have had a much easier time finding work over the years.

"You bet," Ollie said simply. He sat forward on his seat again, and looked him right in the eye. "The biggest thing: Networking. And you're doing it. It's a domino effect. One thing leads to another." He picked up his coffee and leaned back. "I'm not proud to admit this, you understand, but it took me 'til last year to start networking at all. I should have been doing it my whole career— even when I was in the service. It has translated to a lot of heartburn and lost time. That's why last year was so bad for me: I neglected meeting new people. And it takes time to do that. And to get on calendars. That, plus I hadn't been in touch with people I *already* knew, like my old army buddies, which put me even further behind. Just so busy trying to live life, you know? But once I started networking, I realized it was good to see old friends and colleagues again. And as I did so, I learned new, important things about my field. Just by catching up. And *that* made me rethink what I was doing. And *that* helped me understand who I needed to network with next. And *that* eventually led me here. Maybe you can see what I mean about the domino effect. It was a real wake-up call. Truth is, had I talked with your aunt *first*, or even been in touch after losing my last job, I might have gotten to this job sooner."

Ray nodded. He could see why meeting with people he knew first would be a good idea. And it was all making him feel much, much better. There were two decades between he and Ollie, but this sounded just like his story.

Now that he was thinking about it, Ray felt relieved that he hadn't let too much time get away from him before networking. If Ollie had a tough time getting a job without networking, Ray was sure it would be even more difficult for him if he waited longer.

"Did networking do anything else for you?" Ray asked, feeling braver now. "I mean besides, you know, seeing friends and helping get you a job?"

"Well, for starters, I have *new* friendships," Ollie replied. "And yes, it's helped my day-to-day work because after meeting so many new people, I've developed a wide network that I use for business and a variety of other things. Sales for our products. New business development that leads to referrals. New business relationships for future partnerships. Even vacation suggestions."

Ray laughed.

Keeping things on track, he moved to his next question. It was the toughest of them all, but he reminded himself of what Ollie just said about getting out there to network.

"You said you developed a wide network," Ray said. "That you kept meeting new people. I'm hoping to do the same—develop a wide network. Do you know others I could connect with as part of my job search? Maybe engineers or professionals connected to the education or medical world?"

Ray braced for the worst. He knew Ollie was willing to lend advice, but he wasn't convinced that he would share names or think he was ready for additional meetings yet. But his question was coming from a place of sincerity. He could only be gracious if he was denied.

"For sure," Ollie said. "Maybe a couple of people around here. I'm not sure if any are going to lead you right to a job, but they know other people, and they know people, too, so—it's a start. I can check." Ollie grinned and wrote a few names on a piece of paper. "And there are a few vets from the event a few weeks back that work as engineers. Talk to them first."

Other veterans, yes. If networking with Ollie was any indication, networking with other veterans who had been back in the civilian world for a longer time, was a great idea.

"Is it alright that I use your name?" Ray asked.

"Yes."

"And can you think of anything else I should be aware of?"

This made Ollie pause and think again.

"Yes. One thing—I wasn't a good question-asker like you seem to be. Just remember: if you wonder something, it means you don't have an answer yet. Don't be afraid to ask the question."

A pearl of wisdom.

Ray thanked Ollie and began putting his things back into his folder. He was done. It felt good, and he was grateful for Ollie's help; enough to be sure this wouldn't be one-sided.

"One more question, Ollie. How can I help *you*?"

Ollie set his coffee on the table. He had never been asked this before.

"I can't think of anything, Ray," he chuckled. "That's a question I wasn't expecting!"

"Well, please think about it," Ray replied. "You're active with youth basketball. Two guys from my unit played in college and now coach kids. Maybe I can help there." He stood and held out his hand. "Or perhaps I can take you to lunch after I've landed a job."

"Where are you going?" Ollie asked with a laugh as he stood and shook it. Ray promised only twenty minutes, but *everyone* said that.

"A promise is a promise," Ray said. "I really appreciate your insights and your referrals, but I mean to let you get back to your day. Plus—I've got lots to do, too! But I'll be in touch again, soon!"

Ollie walked around the table. He was impressed with the way Ray handled himself and this meeting.

"Well, I'm glad I could help. I think we covered some good ground."

"Before I go," Ray said, opening his bag. "I wanted to give this to you as a token of thanks." It was a copied magazine article about hunting dogs. "The last time I saw you, I remember you mentioning dog training. I happened to read this article, and thought you might like what the author has to say."

Ollie beamed as he thumbed through the article. It was a big expression of thanks, especially since he hadn't expected anything at all. More impressive was that Ray had remembered something that was dear to Ollie—sporting dogs had been part of his family for generations.

"It's very thoughtful of you, Ray. Thank you!"

Ollie's smile told Ray everything he needed to know about this meeting. It had gone right, and he had done a good job, even in spite of his reservations. It meant that with some practice, he could do this over and over again. Things were looking up.

"Thanks again for your time, Ollie. I'll be in touch again after I've met with your colleagues. Have a good day!"

Q&A with
Ray Burke:
"How did it go for you?"

What did you do to plan for your *20-Minute Networking Meeting*?

I looked up Ollie on LinkedIn and was surprised by some things I didn't know about him. Like being connected to my aunt's friend, Andre, through youth basketball. When I asked Andre about it, he encouraged me to reach out. It was a coincidence running into Ollie at the alumni event, as Ollie had moved after getting a new job. But I felt my earlier homework had prepared me for the chance meeting.

How did the meeting itself go for you?

Great. I think I was clear about my military experience, and what I was looking to do with it. And I liked knowing that I felt respected for staying on track, too. In a way, Ollie seemed to really respect that I was keeping to my word about that. Better yet, I got all the information I needed to continue my networking, and I have a feeling of optimism that I can do this networking thing.

Was twenty minutes long enough?

Definitely. Ollie was actually asking for more time! I was still able to tell him about my background and what I was looking for. In that time, we were also able to cover a couple of other topics, including his thoughts on networking.

What do you think Ollie got out of it?

A new respect for me. I can be pretty introverted, and he saw a different me. Plus he's been in this position; I know that he knows it's hard. Seeing that I was willing to ask for help was a big deal. Also, before the meeting, I think Ollie probably thought I wanted to get a job just anywhere. Telling him I was interested in something specific that would help others and help me grow was probably something he didn't know. It was good to clarify that point. It gives direction to my search, and helps me avoid accepting a job just for the sake of getting a job.

How do you plan to follow up?

I plan to send Ollie an email today, thanking him for his time. I might also reiterate my willingness to help with youth basketball. I'll definitely let him know when I've made contact with the people he referred me to. He should know that I took advantage of what he offered me, and that I didn't waste his twenty minutes.

Is there anything you would do differently next time?

I'll stay more open about these meetings. I won't be as nervous. Only good things can come out of them—definitely nothing bad. At the very worst, nothing will happen at all. And if time is not an issue for my contacts, I may let the meetings go longer.

Q&A with Ollie Trent: "How did it go for you?"

What did you like about Clint's *20-Minute Networking Meeting*?

Ray and I have known each other for a long time, but I like that he was still considerate about my time. So many networking meetings are just long social sessions that don't get to the point. Maybe it's because it feels good to be in something like a business meeting, I don't know. But that's no excuse for disrespecting the time of others, and Ray didn't do that.

He also had things to talk about. He was prepared with things to discuss, and he knew a lot about my new company. And he did a great job talking about his military experience and what he wanted to do with that. Speaking as a veteran, that's big and I instantly thought of others that could help him because of it. Also, he had thought ahead of time about what I could add to his job search, and he had some good questions lined up. I liked that. Plus, he brought me an article about dogs. That was not necessary, but thoughtful. I can't believe he remembered that conversation.

Now I'll remember that he remembered.

Was it long enough?

Actually, not quite! I was literally left wanting more. I would have enjoyed talking to him for longer, but I know he's serious about his job hunt and has a lot to get done. If he gets back to me about how his meetings go with the people I set him up with, we'll probably get more time to catch up. Besides, I'm going to forward his information to another guy I know. We'll probably end up talking about that, too.

Were you expecting anything that didn't happen in this meeting?

I was expecting it to be longer and less structured. Networking meetings seem to be conversations where people want to just chat—a get-to-know-you session. This was different, and it surprised me, but in a good way. Ray had a plan, which he stuck to, and he actually led the meeting. That was a first. I was surprised that all I had to do was sit back and help where I could. Which is the whole point, I suppose. Now I've learned something, too.

Is there anything you would change about the meeting?

Nothing about this meeting, in particular. But, I suppose there could be flexibility at times, to be longer. If I was meeting with a friend or former co-worker that I had not seen in years, we might need more than twenty minutes to catch up. On the other hand, I suppose the catching up part can be separate.

The End

You now have all the tools necessary for a new—and different—kind of job search. Take time to hone them. Make them yours. While the intent was to create a simple and straightforward model incorporating the best of what we have seen in the most effective networking meetings, it will be up to you to personalize your style and make things work in your favor. All it takes is the commitment and desire to make it happen.

As we part ways (for now), here are a few things to remember.

- **Networking is more than important. It is *vital*.** It is the lifeblood of your job search and, in the big picture, your career.
- **Networking meetings don't have to be complicated.** Your simple objectives for each meeting are to learn a little, gain an additional contact or two, and hopefully, create an evangelist. If it doesn't happen in one meeting, don't dwell on it. Modify what needs to be changed and try to make it happen at the next. Remember, networking is a skill that can be *learned* and perfected with practice.

- **Networking meetings, like *any* meeting, have a beginning, middle, and end.** Remember that since you called the meeting, it will be up to you to manage where it stands. Be clear about the start, and once you've finished your brief and meaningful discussion, be clear about the end.
- **Throughout each of your discussions, you will be displaying your preparedness,** your organizational skills, your focus, and your genuine interest in the other person. Make it count. How well you do this will define the impression that you leave your contact with, which partly decides if they become an evangelist.
- **Networking is give-and-take!** Reciprocate, and always be prepared with something to give back. It is an opportunity to continue to serve others for their serving you.
- **Last but not least, *you have flexibility*.** I was careful to mention throughout the book that 20 minutes is merely a guideline. Networking, after all, is a people activity. Things jump off agenda, and topics take turns. This can be a good thing, as side-tracked conversation can lead to more information. But remember to use judgment. If you get the sense that your meeting has strayed from the focus of your objectives, just get back on track!

That's it. *Fin! Finito!* The world is now your oyster. Take it. Own it. Make it yours!

We wish you the best as you hit the networking circuit and hope that your new experiences show immediate and permanent changes to your career objectives. Have faith and trust in others. Without a doubt, positive change will come, and with it, the next solid step in your career!

APPENDIX

Your 20-Minute Networking Meeting Cheat Sheet

Print or tear this page out. Mark it. Use it as a guideline. Pace your house and be sure you know its order and its content. Once you have it locked down, figure out where there can be flexibility, and allow yourself to develop it.

Congratulations on finishing *The 20-Minute Networking Meeting*. Now go get started!

STEP 1:	Great First Impression
TIME LIMIT:	*2–3 minutes: thanks and chitchat*
STEP 2:	Great Veteran Overview
TIME LIMIT:	*1 minute overview of experience*
STEP 3:	Great Discussion
TIME LIMIT:	*12–15 minutes: 5 key questions*
STEP 4:	Great Ending
TIME LIMIT:	*2 minutes: thanks and wrap-up*
STEP 5:	Great Follow-Up
TIME LIMIT:	*Meaningful follow-up, right after the meeting*

The Readiness Exercise

(Or: Take This Little Test to See If You're Ready)

Take twenty minutes to answer the following questions. Think through each answer before you write. This is not a race. It's about bringing focus to what you don't know about yourself yet. The purpose is to help you get grounded in what you bring to each networking interaction. Your answers can be used as an indicator of your readiness to get into the civilian job market. Don't stop here, however. You can continue to learn the steps of your *20-Minute Networking Meeting*, just be sure you have solid answers to the following questions before you begin any actual networking. Good luck!

The Readiness Exercise

1. What aspects of your work are you really, really good at? For guidance: What experience do you have that others with your background don't? What gets you the most compliments? What do you do faster, better than others?

_____

_____

_____

_____

2. What personality traits do you bring to the workplace? What characteristics have been praised by others? (i.e. efficient; innovative; strategic; communicative; adaptable; etc.) What aspects of your style have been particularly valued?

Now is probably a great time to dust off any personality or leadership-style inventories or assessments you may have taken in the past (such as Myers-Briggs or StrengthsFinder, or perhaps any from the service). If you don't have a recent assessment, it would be a good idea to take one or more now. These things are easily found on the web, or through career counselors. Alternatively, you could ask some of your contacts for their perspective on this question. These might include family, friends, family friends, former classmates, or service colleagues and peers. (_Don't be afraid to ask. They'll see that you're doing the kind of homework that you should be doing._)

_____

_____

_____

3. What specific areas of expertise do you have that others don't? (Even if you don't have a lot of professional experience, think of what separates you from others who have the same or similar experience that you have.)

_____

_____

_____

_____

4. Are you aware of how your service skills transfer to the civilian workforce?

☐ Yes   ☐ No

5. Do you know how to translate and articulate those skills in civilian terms?

☐ Yes   ☐ No

6. What specific areas of expertise do you have that others don't? (Even if you don't have a lot of professional experience, think of what separates you from others who have the same or similar experience that you have.)

_____

_____

_____

_____

7. Complete the following sentence:

"An organization would be fortunate to have me join them as

*(job role)*_____

because _____

_____

_____

_____ . "

8. Respond to the following sentence: "Even though the above is true, I am still working on developing myself in the following areas." (This is where the perspectives of your contacts in Question 2 come in handy.) _____

_____

_____

_____

_____

9. What else makes you a unique job candidate? (International experience; special training or certifications; early professional experience; languages; recognizable programs or group memberships; etc.)

_____

_____

_____

_____

10. I am highly confident and ready going into my job search.
☐ Yes   ☐ No

11. I have the resources (Internet access; money for buses/trains; fees; resumes copies; etc.) to make my job search a great experience.
☐ Yes   ☐ No

DONE. Now take a ten-minute break and review your answers. Do they reflect what you *really* think and feel? Being sure you are rock-solid with these answers is what's going to give you confidence in your networking meetings. Don't rush it. And come back to this worksheet to revise your answers as you find a better way to express yourself.

The Great First
Impression Planner

Here's a quick worksheet to help you figure out your game plan and how to make a solid first impression. Feel free to tear this out and fill it in if that's best for you.

WHAT YOU'RE GOING TO DO:

Take twenty minutes to answer these questions after setting up a meeting. Recheck your responses for any opportunity to tweak the answers or strengthen your information.

- **Arrival** *(Early, but not **too** early!)*
- **Where are we meeting?** *(Make sure this is established.)*
- **What's the address?** *(Make sure you're sure.)*
- **Do I know how to get there?** *(Be darned positive. You don't want to be late due to construction, weather, traffic, location parking, flat tire, or the odd traffic ticket.)*

FIRST IMPRESSIONS

If meeting at the contact's office, do I know the dress code, if any?
☐ Yes ☐ No

(**NOTE:** *If in doubt, ask a colleague or someone at the office's* *front desk. It's not a bad question to ask. Better yet, come dressed professionally. If you're a jobseeker, the last impression you want to leave is that you were more casually dressed than your contact.)*

Do I know how to pronounce the contact's name correctly?
☐ Yes   ☐ No
(Boy, do we see and hear this one a lot. It's hard to help someone who doesn't even know your name. It's also hard to get past the embarrassment when you screw it up.)

SETTING THE AGENDA
Have you planned your agenda?
☐ Yes   ☐ No

Do you know your five key questions? (Go back to *Step 3 — Great Discussion* if you don't recall this part.)
☐ Yes   ☐ No

HIGHLIGHTING CONNECTIONS
Have I done my research in order to make great connections?

☐ Read the contact's company website.

☐ Read personal bios available on the organization's website.

☐ Reviewed contact's LinkedIn profile; noted any connections in common.

☐ Did a web search; noted any outside board positions; interests; things in common; etc.

☐ Reviewed any armed services background the contact may have

☐ Jotted down key connections to mention in your *20-Minute Networking Meeting.*

The One-Minute Great Veteran Overview Planner

Okay, here's how you put together your one-minute veteran overview.

WHAT TO DO:

- Print a copy of your resume; DD Form 214; Certificate of Release; or Discharge from Active Duty papers
- Decide what stands out or what you want to focus on
- Mark or highlight those items (You'll be highlighting the most important features of your background that make you unique, as we've explained them in Step 2 - Great Veteran Overview.)
- Find five to ten things in total (Shoot for five at the very least.) Here are some possibilities:
  - Your current position
  - Size and scope of your current responsibilities
  - Your prior position(s), summarized
  - Any education or special certifications

IMPORTANT: This list is meant to *complement* Step 2 — Great Veteran Overview, not replace it! Use that Chapter to build your Great Overview, and use this list to augment it.

WHAT TO DO NEXT:

- Compile these key points on another document
- Read through the points out loud
- Time it. If it takes around one minute out loud, perfect; you've got your one-minute overview. If you're over, trim the fat and keep the most important points.
- If you're too short of a minute, add another point or leave it as-is if you feel good about it
- Finally, string it all together using your own words (Also known as "making it yours"). Take your time. Make it fluid and easy to understand. Done.

A QUICK REVIEW

Here, reworded, is the structure for your One-Minute Overview:

- Tally your years in your particular job function, and/or in the armed services
- Highlight your background (civilian and/or service)
- Follow with where you've worked (civilian and/or service)

Now string them all together in a sentence or two (three or more will work, too—just stick with one minute). *Voilà!* One-minute Great Veteran overview!

<><><><><><><><><><><><><><><><><><><><><><><><><><><><><><><><><><><><><><>

TIP

Don't feel like you have to nail this thing in an afternoon. As you continue to work on your networking game plan, come back to it and rehearse it a few more times. This will help you learn your material in a natural way, rather than forcing the words to come out like a business pitch. Again, *make it your own*, take your time, and don't force anything.

Your Small Token of Gratitude

(Actual *Things You Can Give in Return*)

The consummate giver in my own network is our colleague Lars, a man who is 100% focused, 24/7, on what he can give to others. He has been cited as the "Most Networked Person in the Twin Cities" by the publication *Minnesota Business*. Lars is mid-30s and the most networked person because other people like knowing him. And they like knowing him because he is a giver at all levels.

Lars shared his philosophy of *giving* as a strategy for jobseekers. Here is a thank-you note that he received (printed with his permission, with names changed to protect anonymity):

Hi, Lars:

I accepted a position at XYZ Corporation and start my new job on Monday! You can read the story in the business publication, but basically I'll be running their national sales and operations. It's a tremendously exciting opportunity and I'm just thrilled (and they are pretty happy, too).

I wanted to send you a heartfelt letter of thanks. You were perhaps the most influential person in my search, which found its true spark when we had coffee together. The idea of using this time to give back was the thesis statement of the last four months. I met more people, had more interesting meetings, made more of a difference, and was happier and more satisfied because of that advice.

My life has been measurably improved and it came from that simple thought: Don't think of what your network can do for you, think about what you can do for your network. And you were the person who sparked that idea, so I owe you a big thank-you.

Signed,

Executive Candidate

There you have it. Giving back will work wonders for you, too.

Here are a few things you can give your contact in return. It never has to be anything big—just something that shows your appreciation.

- **Contact names.** This is a great one. Think about people in your own network that your contact might want to meet, and offer to make introductions. Just as you are reading this material, to learn how to achieve the assistance of others, *others* are in need of assistance of others, too. You can be that person, or the one who connects them.

  NOTE: Remember that *every* person you know is a contact. Finding common ground between two people is the connector. You have more of a network than you realize!

- **Information.** Find up-to-date information on your contact's industry or functional area. If your intelligence gathering uncovers this person's hobbies or interests (such as animal rights, environmentalism, or the clarinet), take related contacts, connections, articles, websites, etc., to the meeting.

- **Potential client ideas.** If the person is a consultant, or related in any way to sales or marketing, he or she would likely be very appreciative of any ideas or referrals that you might have for possible clients or customers. Even if your referral doesn't pan out in a sale, it will still be appreciated.

- **An actual gift.** We understand that not everyone has budget room to spend on gifts, but there are inexpensive, and free alternatives, too. Perhaps a gift card to a coffee chain for an especially helpful contact. Maybe some chocolates. We've seen everything from restaurant gift cards and children's toys (it's a long story) to decorative mini-art pieces and invitations to interesting professional and cultural events.

◇◇◇

TIP

Post-holiday sales can be a boon, as can purchasing items in bulk. One enterprising young networker showed his appreciation by sending me hand-tied fly fishing flies marked with which streams to use them on. If *you* have such arts and crafts experience, you could do this too and save yourself a lot of money! What if all else fails? Do a web search for great inexpensive gift ideas! (And never feel obligated to buy a trick pony or cruise tickets. *Nothing huge!*)

◇◇◇

◇◇◇

TIP

Ultimately, your small token of gratitude could be part of Question 5 in Step 3 ("How can I help *you?*"). More specifically, if your contact is caught by surprise and hasn't given thought as to how you could return the gift of time, your token of gratitude would work well here. Alternatively, your small token of gratitude could be something you send at a later time, too. But not too late—you wouldn't want your contact to feel like an afterthought. Be prompt!

◇◇◇

The Great Discussion Planner

This section is a summary of the five key questions. Using it, take twenty minutes to plan a great discussion, and use it as a quick reference for future conversations.

QUESTIONS 1–3
(THREE UNIQUE QUESTIONS)

Think about what you know about this networking contact. What information is this person uniquely able to give you? The questions are structured as follows:

> **Fact about Contact (Observation)**
> *followed by*
> **Follow-Up Question (Related Question)**

Here are the breakdowns followed by their full approach:

KEY QUESTION - EXAMPLE 1:

Fact about Contact (Observation):
You've been out of the Navy for four years now, and working in manufacturing operations.

Follow-Up Question (Related Question):
Is it much different than the operations work you were doing in the service?

FULL APPROACH:

"You've been out of the Navy for four years now, and working in manufacturing operations. Is it much different than the operations work you were doing in the service?"

KEY QUESTION - EXAMPLE 2:

Fact about Contact (Observation):
You participated in an international interpreter exchange program.

Follow-Up Question (Related Question):
How did that help develop your career? Is it a good idea for someone of my experience?

FULL APPROACH:

"You participated in an international interpreter exchange program. How did that help develop your career? Is it a good idea for someone of my experience?"

KEY QUESTION - EXAMPLE 3:

Fact About Contact (Observation):
You graduated from automotive mechanic school.

Follow-Up Question (Related Question):

With what you learned about repair and mechanics in the Air Force, is it an advantage?

FULL APPROACH:

"You graduated from automotive mechanic school. With what you learned about repair and mechanics in the Air Force, is it an advantage?"

YOUR TURN—QUESTIONS 1–3

Observation: _____

Related Question: _____

_____

Observation: _____

Related Question: _____

_____

Observation: _____

Related Question: _____

_____

QUESTION 4: OTHER CONTACTS

You can use the following question exactly as written, or modify it slightly to your style. No matter how you phrase it, you must ask for additional referrals.

"Is there someone else you know (from your veteran group; trade group; Chamber; industry organization; current company; alumni association, etc.) that I might talk with as I network?"

Your Turn — Question 4 _____

QUESTION 5: HOW CAN I HELP YOU?

Again, you can use the following question exactly as written, or modify it slightly to your style. No matter how you phrase it, just *be sure to ask* how you can help in return.

*"You have been so helpful to me. How can I help **you**?"*

Your Turn — Question 5 _____

The Great
Follow-Up Tracker

WHAT TO DO

Take twenty minutes to follow up after each networking meeting. Here are the steps, laid out for you.

Contact name _____

Business _____

Date _____

FOLLOW UP WITH THE NETWORKING CONTACT

1. Send a brief thank-you to the networking contact. (They met with you to help you.)
   ☐ Done
2. Send a brief thank-you to the person who referred you to that contact. (They referred you to help you.)
   ☐ Done
3. Add any new or updated information about this person to your networking database. (Track *everything*.)
   ☐ Done
4. Make a note to follow up with this contact, as appropriate.
☐ Done

FOLLOW UP WITH YOURSELF

1. What did you do well?_____

_____

_____

2. What will you do differently next time? _____

_____

_____

3. What did you learn and how will you apply that information?

_____

_____

_____

FOLLOW UP WITH NEW CONTACTS

1. What names of future contacts did you get?

_____

_____

2. Schedule follow-up with each of these new contacts.
   ☐ Done

Skills Translation & Career Transition Resources

Here is a shortlist of resources to help you kickstart service-to-civilian skills-translation. It is *not* a comprehensive list, but has links to each branch of the armed services for those in current transition, and links to other websites for those who aren't.

Also included are links to websites where you can obtain government service documents that outline your past military experience and training. (Using *any* of these is a solid first step to your skills recollection and translation.)

Please Note: Due to the ever-evolving nature of hyperlinks and webpage administration, these links may change or lead to Page Does Not Exist errors. If this happens, try searching from the home page of that website.

COLLECT YOUR RESUME MATERIAL

DEPARTMENT OF DEFENSE - Get a copy of your Verification of Military Experience and Training.
https://www.dodtap.mil/login.html

NATIONAL PERSONNEL RECORDS CENTER - Get a copy of your DD-214; Certificate of Release or Discharge from Active Duty, which outlines last duty assignment and rank; Military job specialty; Military education.
https://www.archives.gov/personnel-records-center/dd-214

LIFE & SKILLS TRANSITION - SEPARATION TRANSITION ASSISTANCE PROGRAMS (TAP)

These links provide information, training and tools to help current members and their families prepare for next steps in civilian life. (These sites also have translator tools in them, and may require registration or logins.)

ARMY
https://www.acap.army.mil/

AIR FORCE
http://www.afpc.af.mil/transition-assistance-program

NAVY
https://www.cnic.navy.mil/ffr/family_readiness/fleet_and_family_support_program/work-and-family-life/transition_assistance.html

MARINE CORP
http://www.usmc-mccs.org/index.cfm/services/career/transition-readiness/

COAST GUARD
http://www.dcms.uscg.mil/our-organization/assistant-commandant-for-human-resources-cg-1/health-safety-and-work-life-cg-11/office-of-work-life-cg-111/transition-assistance-program/

TRANSLATION TOOLS

O*Net Online Crosswalk Search - Translator & Skills Matching
https://www.onetonline.org/crosswalk/MOC/

Military.com - Military Skills Translator
https://www.military.com/veteran-jobs/skills-translator

Military Connection - MOS Translator
https://militaryconnection.com/military-skills-translator/

CareerOneStop - sponsored by the U.S. Dept. of Labor - Skills Translator
https://www.dol.gov/veterans/findajob/

Military to Federal Jobs Crosswalk - Translator & Federal Jobs
http://www.dllr.state.md.us/mil2fedjobs/

OTHER RESOURCES

U.S. Department of Veterans Affairs - Vocational Rehabilitation and Employment (VR&E). You can apply for career and education counseling here.
https://www.benefits.va.gov/vocrehab/index.asp

RallyPoint
From the website: "RallyPoint is the premiere digital platform for the military community to come together and discuss military topics both socially and professionally."
https://www.rallypoint.com/about-us

Congratulations—
you've learned to network.
Now go get that job!

About the Authors

Nathan A. Perez is an executive career coach at Career Innovation, and is publisher at Career Innovations Press.

A 14-year veteran of the retained executive search industry, Nathan worked in the Research function. Responsible for the first step in the executive recruitment process, Nathan's main responsibility was to find the (qualified) candidates to recruit. He has been cited by *The Huffington Post* as one of the most connected people on LinkedIn world-wide.

Co-author of the acclaimed job-search networking book *The 20-Minute Networking Meeting*, Nathan speaks to students, career coaches, executives and veterans across the country, in person and guest webinars. An enthusiastic and hands-on coach, Nathan helps strengthen the presence of his job-searching clients by combining his executive search experience with years in front of cameras and on stage. A formally trained actor, Nathan spent 20 years in New York City and Hollywood as a professional performer and writer.

Nathan is a professional member of the Authors Guild; the National Speakers Association; Actors Equity Association (AEA); and a voting union member of The Screen-Actors Guild (SAG-AFTRA). He is a former Vice Chair of the Board at The Loft Literary Center, one of the nation's leading literary arts centers, and is an Honorary Commander of 934th Airlift Wing, United States Air Force Reserve, home of the "Global Vikings."

www.nathanaperez.com

Marcia Ballinger is a Co-Founder and Principal at Ballinger|Leafblad, a St. Paul-based executive search firm focused on serving the civic sector. She conducts executive search projects for top executives in non-profit organizations, higher education, foundations and professional associations. A frequent presenter to groups of executives, Marcia is widely known as a no-nonsense representative of the executive search industry.

Marcia has a BS in Business Administration and an MA in Speech-Communication along with a PhD in Organization and Management from Capella University where she served on the Board of Directors. She is active in a variety of non-profit organizations and was named an Industry Leader by the Minneapolis/St. Paul Business Journal in 2008; Real Power 50 by Minnesota Business Monthly; and 50 Over 50 by AARP in 2016.

She lives with her husband and dogs in St. Paul, Minnesota.

Made in the USA
Monee, IL
28 October 2023

45349388R00111